Bulletin Board Basics
Hands-On Science

by
Jeannine Perez

Art by
Nina Gaelen,
Catherine Minor,
Debby Dixler

FIRST TEACHER PRESS
First Teacher, Inc./Bridgeport, CT

ISBN 1-878727-09-5

Cover and Page Design: Gene Krackehl
Cover photo: Andrew Brilliant and Carol Palmer (taken at Care A Lot Childcare Center, Lexington, MA)
Cover Color: Lisa Schustak

Edited by Helen Strahinich, Eric Hogan
Editorial Assistant: Beth Gordon
Art Editor: Debby Dixler
Typesetting and Layout: Anita Golton, Beth Ann Bogert

Special thanks to Thomas Jenen, Alyssa Levy, and Jessica Rubenstein.

Published by First Teacher Press, First Teacher, Inc.
P.O. Box 29, 60 Main Street, Bridgeport, CT 06602

TABLE OF CONTENTS

INTRODUCTION

The prospect of filling empty bulletin boards was always a little bit scary for me—until I learned what makes a successful bulletin board display. In the past, the time and effort required to conceive and maintain bulletin boards seemed formidable. By default, I usually let children post whatever pictures interested them wherever they could reach. As a result, my bulletin boards were uninteresting and sloppy.

Then one day I read the book *Swimmy* by Leo Lionni (Pantheon) to my class. My children were fascinated by the story and dazzled by the illustrations. Not only did they want to hear the story again and again, but they also wanted to see and learn more about the ocean. I took a chance and suggested that we create a marine bulletin board. The results were fabulous. The children made suggestions for the display and for other sea projects. They loved helping to make the board and were engaged by all the projects.

Through that experience, I learned that a successful bulletin board display is *alive*. This vitality stems from children's interest and participation. The displays are exten-sions of our personalities, so they are as interesting as the children themselves.

Let Your Bulletin Board Work for You

The key to a lively bulletin board display is your children's role in its creation. Through children's involvement, it becomes a learning aid and an important teacher resource.

● **Use the board with teaching units.** When children help create bulletin board displays, they make connections between the abstract ideas of the unit and the concrete objects on the board. In the process, they apply and master their new knowledge from the unit.

● **Let the board affect the atmosphere.** A lively, flamboyant, colorful board reflecting your children's personalities makes the classroom welcome and attractive.

● **Give your imagination free rein.** Don't limit yourself or the board—creativity thrives when there are no boundaries. No two bulletin boards are ever alike. Even traditional themes can take on new dimensions when matched to the interests and personalities of your class.

Developing a Bulletin Board Display

Even the most creative and spontaneous activities require some preparation and organization. To make the process of creating your display easier and more fun, you should:
- know your children and their interests well;
- have a goal in mind when you choose a theme for your display;
- sketch an image of the display. Regard it only as a starting point, though—your children may have more ideas than you do!

Preparation

To create a bulletin board display, regardless of the theme, you will need some basic tools and materials:
- a sharp pair of scissors,
- a yardstick or ruler,
- an exacto knife or mat knife,
- a stapler that opens to staple on walls,
- heavy-duty markers,
- newspapers,
- a scrap box with colorful paper, textured fabrics, trims, string, and yarn.

Gather all the materials you think you will need—make sure you have more than enough—to stimulate children's imagination and creativity. In addition to paper and fabrics, use objects and materials with unusual, shapes, colors, or textures that invite children to touch and explore.

Background

A background gives the bulletin board depth and vitality. You can cover the board partially or entirely for a dramatic effect. Use a variety of materials such as wrapping paper, magazine pictures, doilies, cheesecloth, fish net, aluminum foil, plywood, or whatever else you can imagine.

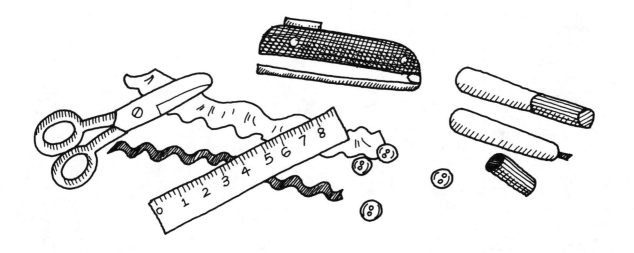

INTRODUCTION

Making Your Display

Now that you have your ideas and materials, you should know the pitfalls to avoid and rules to follow when making your display:

● **Control your bulletin board.** Each display should center on one theme. Don't clutter the board, and don't let the background detract from the main display. When in doubt, leave the extras out and let what *is* on the board show up clearly.

● **Involve your children.** Start by getting on your knees and viewing the scene from a child's perspective. Focal points that are too high are lost on children.

A pegboard or a detachable bulletin board may be removed from the wall and placed on the floor so children have easier access to the display during the decorating process. You can also use a screen or a pegboard as a traveling bulletin board which can be used as a backdrop in different areas of the room.

For large bulletin boards, let children help you plan the display and create the components, which you then put up on the board. If possible, lower your bulletin board until the bottom touches the floor, so that children can decorate the display themselves. Encourage children to participate in all aspects of the display's creation. Watch children's reactions to different parts of the display. Replace those parts that don't interest them with things they would like to see.

Include children's artwork in the display to make it more personal and, therefore, more appealing.

● **Be innovative.** The color of the sky in your display does not always have to be blue. Grass should not always be green. Look at impressionist paintings to learn how color is used to create moods and impressions. Also, displays should not always be two dimensional. Use various textures, materials, and three-dimensional objects to animate your display. You can also use alternative display areas, such as doorways, windows, mobiles, bookcases, table-and-wall areas, and so on. Use your imagination.

Special Effects

It takes more than an interesting theme to make a good display. Capture children's attention with displays that appeal to the senses and invite exploration. Here are some ideas for attention-getters:

- **Create a three-dimensional effect.** Frame or mat pictures on the bulletin board with contrasting or checkered paper, ribbon, aluminum pie plates, etc. To make objects stand out, glue them to small pieces of pleated paper before attaching them to the bulletin board.

- **Create sensory attractions.** Make "smelling bags" out of fabrics that won't rip easily, filling them with items that have interesting scents (pine needles, a handkerchief sprayed with perfume, orange peels, etc.). Make a "touching board" with strips of sandpaper, satin, plastic, etc., so children can feel the different textures.
- **Make an "artist file."** Pin onto the bulletin board folders containing poems, notes, magazine pictures, and pictures created by children.

Balance and Composition

Use a combination of large and small objects, photos, and shapes. Pictures can be displayed in a line or at angles to one another. Geometric shapes make exciting patterns for your display; they draw the eyes and capture children's interest. Make sure you do not have too many big or small things on the board, or your display may seem unbalanced. Above all, keep your display simple. Remember, a cluttered board is a sloppy board.

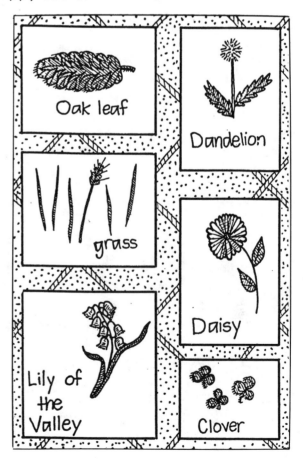

Lettering Your Bulletin Board Display

Words on your display can do more than label and explain. The lettering itself can be an enjoyable and attractive part of the board.

● **Be innovative with your lettering.** You can buy lettering and stencils from a stationery store. However, it's less expensive and more exciting to create letters from a variety of materials, such as yarn, pipe cleaners, rubber bands, colored paper, letters cut from old greeting cards, and so on. Add borders or shadows to your letters to make them more dramatic. If your theme has anything to do with temperature, make your letters appear to melt or to be encased in ice. Have the letters wind through your display or form geometric shapes.

● **Vary the function of your lettering.** Use letters and words in imaginative ways. Have captions cover the board. Cut windows in the letters so that children can discover a photo that is under the window flaps. Or cover the display with an oversized caption and remove one letter or piece of the caption each day. Children will enjoy seeing what is revealed daily and guessing at what is still covered.

Bordering Your Display

Borders frame and focus children's attention on objects in your display. You can buy borders in many colors and designs, but it is more fun to make your own. Border all four sides, or just frame one or two sides. The number of different frames you can make is endless—here are a few suggestions:

● Find pieces of paper with dimensions larger than the object you want to frame. Fold them in half and cut shapes into them.

● Use strips of wallpaper, holiday garlands, rope, or twine.

● Twist ribbon or crepe paper for a holiday or celebration display.

● Place cut-out or stamped hand, foot, or paw prints around the border.

● Make borders with rough, torn, or singed edges to catch children's attention.

Breaking Down Your Bulletin Board Display

Creative displays deserve proper storage. Don't dispose of your favorite display—storing certain elements of the display will save you time and effort the next time you cover its theme.

● Keep your ideas in a notebook, or jot them down on 3" by 5" file cards.

● Take pictures of your most successful displays, and file them.

● If you can, laminate portions of your display, roll them up, and store them.

● Store caption lettering in manila envelopes with the caption written on the front of each envelope.

Each unit in this book opens with a picture of a finished bulletin board. This picture is not meant as a model for you to copy, but as an example from which you can develop your own ideas and projects. The introduction for each unit will suggest what time of year or which specific issues might lend themselves to the general subject of each bulletin board. These units are only meant as springboards for your own creativity and for the creativity of your children.

Creating the Bulletin Board

This section gives you some guidelines concerning the actual construction of the bulletin board, including the background, the border, and the contents of the bulletin board.

Interactions

Children enjoy the bulletin boards much more when they are able to participate in the construction and maintenance. This section provides activities that you and your children can do with the bulletin board display, such as making items to be displayed or discussing the things children can see or touch on the board. These activities allow children to interact directly with the bulletin board.

Making Connections

This section connects the bulletin board themes with other areas of your curriculum. There are learning activities in the following categories:
• Art,
• Cooking,
• Dramatic Play/Creative Movement,
• Language Development,
• Math,
• Music,
• Science.

There are also suggestions for field trips, lists of books, and other resources that might be appropriate for the unit.

Adult supervision is critical for activities which warrant it. Help children with cutting, stapling, and hanging. Teach them how to use scissors and other tools properly. Develop a list of safety rules with them (never run with scissors, always wash hands after using materials, etc.) Use non-toxic supplies, crayons, markers, paints, glue, etc. Use good judgement—several of the activities in this book require the use of small or potentially dangerous items, and are not suitable for children under four years of age. Make safety your first priority at all times.

The activities in this book can be modified to fit your teaching style as well as the interests and personalities of the children in your class. Make each bulletin board uniquely your own, tapping your creative abilities as well as those of your children. Constructing each bulletin board should be an enjoyable learning experience, so have fun!

IN AND AROUND THE SEA

This unit develops children's awareness of the sea as a habitat for many types of plants and animals, including fish, birds, and amphibians. It also demonstrates the role that people play in using and protecting the sea and its inhabitants. This bulletin board can be used to focus children's attention on pollution and on our responsibility to the environment.

Background

Cover the top half of the bulletin board with pale blue paper to look like the sky. Cover the bottom half of the board with deep turquoise-colored paper to look like the sea. You can also make the background with tissue paper or gift wrap. Or help children to brush a dark blue watercolor wash on sheets of newsprint for the sea and a paler shade for the sky. Add a thick strip of brownish-yellow paper or paint across the middle of the board to create a shoreline.

Border

Make the border on the upper half of the board out of fluffy cotton or tissue paper clouds. On the lower half, make the border out of abstract waves cut out by children.

Bulletin Board

Help children fill the board with sea creatures, birds, and boats. Help them paste plants, shells, and rocks made of construction paper to the sea bottom. Use picture books to inspire and to motivate children to create their own imaginary creatures.

● Help children cut out jellyfish and octopus shapes from coffee filters that they have decorated. Let them put these on the board, with the octopods resting on the bottom of the sea and the jellyfish floating on top of the water.

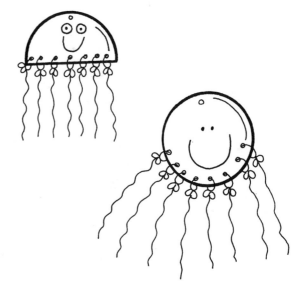

● Cut starfish shapes from cardboard. Let children cover these with glue and then sprinkle them with cornmeal or sand. Staple or glue the starfish to the bulletin board, so that they appear to be lying on the shore or floating on the sea.

● Help children make eels from unwound paper-towel tubes. Let them decorate the tubes with paint and markers. Add these to the bulletin board display.

CREATING THE BULLETIN BOARD

- Cut fish shapes from sponges. Then let children dip the sponges in tempera paint and stamp fish directly onto the board.
- Let children help glue real shells on the display or tie string around shells. Hang these from tacks on the board.
- Help children make a coral reef with vividly colored paper or fabric. Explain to children and then display on the bulletin board how fish use the coral for shelter and protection by hiding in the branches of the reef.
- Help children to cut out white sea gulls from simple patterns you have made and to put them on the board. Have them display the sea gulls swooping down to pluck fish from the sea for dinner, or flying into the clouds.

- Help children make three-dimensional birds and sea creatures from strips of paper that are rolled, bent, and stapled into shape; these will add depth to your bulletin board.

- Let children draw and cut out colorful boats from construction paper—sail boats, fishing boats, row boats, motor boats, and so on. Remind children to draw people on the boats—people in bathing suits, fishing, paddling, racing, etc.

● As you read your class books about ocean life, revise and adapt the bulletin board. *Swimmy* by Leo Lionni (Pantheon) is a good springboard for starting the unit. After you have read the story, help children to cut out shapes of small fish and to put them in the outline of a giant fish on the bulletin board. This actively illustrates the theme of cooperation that children read about in *Swimmy*.

● Use the bulletin board to generate ideas for creative play. Children can pretend to be "Swimmy" or other sea creatures. Make up stories with children about a typical day at the bottom of the sea. Also, have children pretend to be seabirds. Ask them what they would eat and where they would sleep. Let children help create experience charts and stories about life at the seashore. Let each child pick a fish or bird and pretend to be that creature, describing what it feels and sees and how it acts.

● Explore with children the concepts "under," "on" and "above." Ask them questions such as, "*What kinds of things do you find under the sea? What would you find on the sea? How many things can you find on the bulletin board that are found above the sea?*"

● Use the bulletin board for a math game. Play "I Spy," having children find the largest or smallest fish and birds of a certain color on the bulletin board. Ask them to count the number of fish or shells in the sea or birds in the sky. Talk with children about the shapes of the sea creatures on the board. Have them find curved and straight lines, corners, circles, etc.

● Have a beach party in your classroom, using your bulletin board as a backdrop. Bring in rugs, large towels, and a small wading pool filled with warm water. Hang mobiles from the ceiling, and place large shells and plant cuttings in containers of water on the floor and on shelves. Ask children to bring straw hats, swim suits, and sunglasses. Play a tape of ocean sounds as children pretend to swim and sunbathe. If possible, add large rocks with interesting shapes and colors to your classroom beach. Children can sit by the rocks and imagine they are at the ocean.

● Go to the library and find books that illustrate different types of life in and around the sea. Create a cozy reading center near the bulletin board with pillows and a basket of books about shells, seabirds, ocean plants, ocean rocks, coral, fish, and boats, as well as people who live by and on the sea.

Art

• Help children create octopods by drawing funny faces on large balloons which **you** blow up for them. Help children glue eight decorated paper strips to each balloon for the tentacles.

• Help each child cut out and decorate two identical fish. Staple each pair of fish together around the edges, leaving an open space. Help children stuff the fish with crumpled pieces of newspaper. Then staple the opening. Repeat this activity making fish of various sizes. Hang them from the ceiling with different lengths of string to make a school of fish.

• After reading *Casper and the Rainbow Bird* by Robin and Inge Hyman (Barrons), help children draw the outlines of large imaginary birds. Let each child decorate a small area of one bird. The results are colorful birds, covered with spots, stripes, and squiggles.

• Take children outside and let them blow bubbles. Watch as the bubbles disappear. Talk with children about how quickly the fragile bubbles either float away or burst. Go inside and help children make "sea foam" bubble prints. Put one-eighth cup of liquid detergent in each of three bowls. Add water and food coloring to each bowl. Let children use straws to blow in the bowls until bubbles rise over the tops. Help them carefully lay a sheet of paper over the bubbles. The resulting prints are delicate and beautiful. Let children use the same paper to make prints from bubbles in all three bowls. This gives the paper a unique rainbow appearance. With small children, who might suck up the detergent, blow the bubbles yourself and let them make the prints.

Science

- Collect as many different types of shells as possible. Let children examine them under a magnifying glass. Teach children the names of some of the more unique shells. If you can find a conch shell, ask children to listen for the sound of the sea when they hold the shell to their ears.

- Help children create sand molds in a sand box or sand table. Help them to make interesting-shaped depressions in dampened sand with their fingers or with sticks, then to carefully pour in slightly thickened plaster of Paris. Let the plaster harden, and remove it from the sand. Be sure not to pour excess plaster of Paris down the sink drain, or you will be calling a plumber to rescue the situation!

- Fill the water table or a large, elevated container with piles of fine and coarse sand. Add shells, scoops, and sifters. Let children compare the textures of the different types of sand and the shells. Also provide scales and measuring cups for children to do their own experiments.

- Start a collection of feathers that children find on walks. Let children sort the feathers into categories such as fluffy, straight, and curved. Let children trace around the feathers and color the shapes.

- Read *Are You My Mother?* by P.D. Eastman (Random House) in class. Help children make binoculars by fastening two cardboard tubes together with rubber bands. Take children on a bird walk. Make sure children only look through their binoculars while they are standing still—safety first. Also bring a real pair of binoculars and an instant developing camera to observe and to record the birds you see.

- Give each child a milk carton, scissors, paper and a few straws, and challenge them to make seaworthy sailboats. Remind children to decorate the sails so that each boat is identifiable. Help children with cutting and pasting. When every child has made a boat, fill a dishpan or the water table, and have races with children, having them blow on the sails to move their boats. Add small weights or marbles to the boats, and see how many each can hold before it sinks. Sail an empty boat and one with weights in it, and see which one goes faster.

MAKING MORE CONNECTIONS

● Help children make bird feeders from milk cartons. Cut an opening in one side of each carton near the bottom, fill each carton with sunflower seeds and cracked corn, and hang the feeders from tree branches. Another option is stringing popcorn and hanging it from a tree branch. Or hollow out half of an orange, fill it with a mixture of cornmeal and peanut butter, and place the orange securely in a tree. Children can also make bird feeders from large pine cones coated in peanut butter and rolled in bird seed or grain. Have children watch for birds at the feeders, and help them record their observations of the birds.

Field Trips

Arrange a visit to an aquarium, pet store, aviary or fish nursery. Devise a "treasures-of-the-sea" hunt as part of the trip. Depending on where you go, have children look for fish that change color, creatures that live in shells, animals that look like plants, or birds that live in trees, in bushes, or on the ground. You can also give children pictures of fish and birds to locate. If you live near a large body of water, plan a visit to a boatyard or a dock. You might even charter a boat for a ride. Another idea is to visit a boat museum or take children to an amusement park or a carnival for the children's boat rides.

Cooking

● **Bird Seed Cookies** Help children sprinkle egg-shaped pieces of packaged cookie dough with colored sugar or poppy seeds. Bake as directed on the package.

● **Fish Cookies** Let children roll small balls and "snakes" out of packaged cookie dough. Let them form the bodies of the fish from the balls, and bend the "snakes" into v-shapes and attach as tails. Decorate the cookies with vegetable-colored poppy seeds, and bake them as directed on the package.

● **Celery Boats** Help children spread peanut butter on celery sticks and put raisins on top as the sailors. Let them add carrot-stick masts and then make the boats "set sail"— right into their mouths!

Math

● Let children sort shells according to size, shape, color, and other characteristics.

● Give children problems to solve such as, "*If a whale's head were here at this tree, and his tail stretched to the fence, how big would he be?*" Have them space the distance with footsteps, body lengths, and other non-standard measurements.

Music

● Substitute sea-animal names in various songs. For example, teach children "My Dolphin Swims Over the Ocean," sung to the tune of "My Bonnie Lies Over the Ocean."

● Teach children the following songs about having fun at the beach:

To the Beach
(tune: "A-Hunting We Will Go")
It's to the beach we go,
We won't find any snow;
We'll swim and float,
And fish from a boat—
I can't wait 'till we go!

Sand
(tune: "The Farmer in the Dell")
Gritty, sticky sand,
Itchy in my clothes,
But feels so soft and cool and smooth
Between my wiggly toes!

Dramatic Play/Creative Movement

● Bring in a large cardboard box, and cut circular "portholes" on the two longest sides. Put several small pillows in the box as life preservers and tell children the box is a boat. Let them float on the sea and talk about what they see.

● Let children pretend to be baby birds talking and playing together in a nest. Help them make bird masks by taking paper bags, trimming them with fringes and feathers, and taping on large beaks made of paper cones.

● Give each child a feather. Ask children to gently blow the feathers and watch their movements in the air. Let children pretend they are feathers, floating in the air and falling to the ground.

Language Development

● Help children dictate a weekly animal newsletter, "Fish and Feather Feature," based on the experience charts they made in "Interactions" (page 11).

● Help children make and illustrate an "In and Around the Sea" riddle book, using riddles you ask them at circletime, such as:

"*Why are fish so smart?*" "*Because they travel in schools.*"

"*What fish tastes best in a sandwich?*" "*A jellyfish.*"

"*What kind of bird eats all the time?*" "*A swallow.*"

● Display rocks in a clear container. Add water and have children list the differences between wet rocks and dry rocks. Let children wash all the rocks in your collection. Have them compare smooth river rocks, rough gravel, and the fine sand at the beach.

● Read stories about snails to children. After doing some research on water snails, purchase some from a pet store. Let each child take a snail home in a baby food jar full of water with holes punched in the lid.

Read Aloud Books

🕮 *Are You my Mother?* by P.D. Eastman (Random House)

🕮 *Birds* by Jane Werner Watson (Golden Books)

🕮 *A Boat for Peppe* by Leo Politi (Scribners)

🕮 *Casper and the Rainbow Bird* by Robin and Inge Hyman (Barron's Woodbury)

🕮 *Fishes* by Brian Wildsmith (Franklin Watts)

🕮 *The Great Fish* by Peter Parnall (Doubleday)

🕮 *If the Sea were Sweet* by Martine Sequin-Fontes (Larousse)

🕮 *In My Boat* by Betsy Maestro (Thomas Y. Crowell)

🕮 *The Mysterious Tadpole* by Stephen Kellogg (Dial Books)

🕮 *One Morning in Maine* by Robert McClosky (Puffin Books)

🕮 *Out to Sea* by Anne and Harlow Rockwell (Macmillan)

🕮 *Snails* by Herbert S. and Lucretia Krantz (William Morrow)

🕮 *Swimmy* by Leo Lionni (Pantheon)

🕮 *The Tiny Patient* by Judy Pederson (Alfred A. Knopf)

🕮 *Three Friends* by Robert Kraus (Windmill Books)

🕮 *Tugboats Never Sleep* by Kathryn Lasky (Little, Brown & Co.)

🕮 *Ugly Bird* by Russell Hoban (Macmillan)

NIGHT AND DAY

This unit encompasses several different subjects: the sun, moon, and stars; animals that sleep during the night and animals that sleep during the day; things that people do during the day and things that they do during the night. This is a wonderful bulletin board to adapt for Halloween, as well, since children can have fun learning about scary noises and creatures of the night while also learning about the activities that go on in the daytime. You could also create a bulletin board exclusively about nighttime, taking the nighttime themes and activities from this unit and combining them with some of your own.

Background

Begin this bulletin board display by dividing the background diagonally or vertically. Make one half the "day" section and the other half the "night" section. The background for the day section should be white and the one for the night section should be gray.

Border

Make the border out of yellow paper. Give the border a scalloped edge by using a glass or saucer as a pattern. Create a window image by hanging a cheesecloth curtain from a rod or from hooks at the top of the board. Alternate closing the drape on the night and day sides of the board.

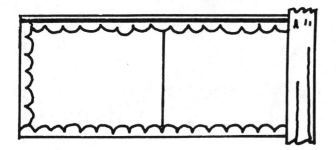

Bulletin Board

● Let children decorate the "day" section of the board with pictures of daytime images and activities, such as a happy yellow sun shining down on pictures of children playing "Ring Around the Rosie." Be sure to include pictures of animals that work and play during the day and plants that need the sun to live.

● The "night" half should be a shadowed landscape. Have children cut or tear silhouettes of trees and houses from black paper. Let them add a night sky with cut-outs of colored stars and a big bright moon. Staple the stars in various places around the moon. Tell children that in real life the moon is not always visible on a starry night. Have them look at the sky one starry night and come in the next day with a description of what they saw.

CREATING THE BULLETIN BOARD

- Help children draw and cut out owl silhouettes with big, round yellow eyes. Paste these in the trees on the night side of the bulletin board.

- Have children cut out and paste on the board pictures of other nocturnal animals—crickets, coyotes, bats—from old issues of *Ranger Rick*, *National Geographic*, and other nature magazines.

- For Halloween, on the day side, have children make cut-outs of themselves dressed in costumes and trick-or-treating. On the night side, emphasize natural spooks rather than goblins, ghosts, and witches. Use the caption "Things that Go Bump in the Night." Use white lettering edged in black, and make the letters spooky, wiggly shapes. Use pictures from magazines or children's drawings of Jack o' Lanterns, bats, cats with big yellow eyes, owls, possums, tree branches that skitter and scrape against windows, and insects such as fire flies and spiders.

● Make houses from two shoe boxes. Cut out windows and doors, and help children decorate the houses—inside and out—with colored paper, paint, and markers. Help them to make cut-outs of furniture, appliances, fireplaces, and furnishings and to glue them in place. Help children draw and cut out people to live in the houses (or use small plastic figures). Staple the houses to the bulletin board, one on the daytime side and one on the nighttime side, low enough so that children can reach them. Give children time to play with the houses, acting out daytime activities in the daytime house and nighttime activities in the nighttime house.

● Using the board as backdrop, have some children act out daytime activities and night-time routines. Have other children guess what the "actors" are pretending to do.

● Give children old magazines, and help them find pictures of daytime and nighttime activities. Have children separate the pictures and paste them onto two file folders, one for day and one for night. Staple the folders to the appropriate sides of the bulletin board. As children find more day and night pictures during the unit, have them add these to the appropriate folder.

INTERACTIONS

● Have children create ghost pictures. Thin down some white tempera paint with water, and pour a small amount into a shallow dish. Help children clip clothespins to stout pieces of string about six inches long. Let them dip the string into the paint and carefully let it drop and dance several times on black sheets of paper. When the paint is dry, have children paint two white eyes wherever they see a rounded "ghost head." You can also use black paint on white paper.

● Tell children that animals which are active during the daytime are called "diurnal" animals, while those which are active during the nighttime are called "nocturnal" animals. Buy or make a recording of the calls made by some of the diurnal and nocturnal animals pictured on the board. Have children try to identify the animals by their calls, and guess whether they are diurnal or nocturnal.

● Help children make nighttime landscapes by drawing trees and houses with white crayons, white tempera paint, or white chalk on dark blue or black paper. Or have children draw a bright daytime picture with crayons on white paper. When the pictures are done, turn some into night scenes by brushing them with thinned down blue or black tempera paint. To make the garden pictures look like dusk scenes, use dark water color washes over the crayon designs.

Art

• Help children create "sunshine art." Give each child a heavy duty sheet of white paper. Then ask children to cut out shapes, such as flowers, houses, and butterflies. Staple each shape to the center of a piece of dark-colored construction paper. Tape the pictures to the inside of a sunny window with the cut-out facing the window. After a few weeks, take down the pictures and remove the shapes. Discuss with children the difference between the color of the sun-faded paper and that of the section blocked from the sunlight.

• Have children color clear plastic can lids with markers. Help them cut out simple shapes (butterflies, circles, triangles, etc.) from the colored lids. Stick the plastic shapes to a sunny window with a few drops of water. Watch the shadows and colors on the walls and floors of the room.

• Help children make "moonburst" paintings by dropping spoonfuls of thinned white and blue paint on slippery black fingerpaint paper. Let children use straws to blow paint into moonburst designs.

MAKING MORE CONNECTIONS

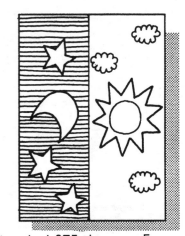

Cooking

● **Breakfast Biscuits** Let children help make baking-powder biscuits from a mix. Knead the dough and form it into balls about an inch in diameter. Dip each ball in melted margarine, and then into a cinnamon-sugar mixture (about 1/4 teaspoon cinnamon to 1/2 cup sugar). Place the balls close together on a baking sheet and bake in a 350-degree oven for 20 to 30 minutes. The baking time depends on the size of the biscuits and how close they are to each other. Let children enjoy eating the biscuits while they are warm.

● **"Midnight" Snack** Flatten biscuit dough to make individual pizza crusts. Spoon a little pizza or spaghetti sauce on each biscuit. Top with shredded mozzarella cheese and bake on a greased cookie sheet at 375 degrees F for 8 to 12 minutes. Provide additional toppings —pepperoni, ground sausage, hamburger, green peppers, mushrooms, black olives, chopped onions, etc.—for "personalized pizzas." Let each child add the toppings she wants before you bake the pizzas.

● **Animal Pancakes** Make animal pancakes for a special breakfast! Use a mix to make the batter. Make sure the batter is fairly thin. When you pour the batter onto the grill, use a wooden spoon to form legs, horns, and other animal features. Birds and bunnies are the easiest to make, but any odd-shaped pancake will remind a child of some kind of animal. Serve the pancakes with strawberries, apple sauce, or honey.

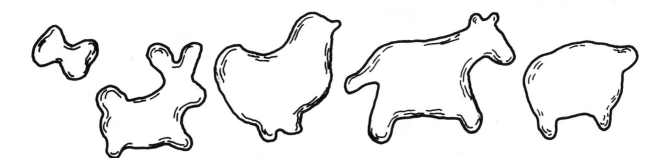

Dramatic Play/Creative Movement

● Play "shadow tag" with children outside when it is sunny. Have children play tag as usual, except that someone becomes "it" when her shadow is stepped on by the current "it."

● On a sunny day, let three or four children stand together in funny positions to create a weird shadow with several arms and legs on the sidewalk outside. Have other children count the arm and leg shadows.

● Read a bedtime story such as *The Moon Jumpers* by Janice May Udry (Harper & Row). Let children pantomime their own bedtime routines. Ask them to include any tactics they can think of to delay their "bedtime." When children are finally ready for "sleep," play soft music and darken the room. After a brief rest, turn on the lights and pull up the shades. Everybody should be energized and ready for more daytime fun!

● Ask children to come to school dressed in their pajamas and slippers. Dress the part yourself. Serve breakfast. In the middle of the day, have a slumber party with bed-time stories and a "midnight" snack.

● Play a circle game. Have one child, holding a large yellow cardboard disk, pretend to be the sun. Have other children stand in a circle with their backs to the middle of the circle. Have the sun walk slowly around the circle. When the children in the circle do not see the sun, they should act out nighttime activities or pretend to sleep. When they can see the sun, they should act out daytime activities.

● Let children dress dolls or stuffed animals in clothes suitable for different daytime and nighttime activities, such as school, parties, and bedtime.

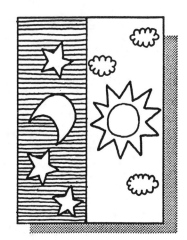

Math

● Make a large monthly calendar from pasteboard. Be sure that the squares for each day are large enough for the date and for comments. During each circletime, mention the year, the month, and the day to children, and let them come up with one important thing about the day. The day's comment could be about the weather ("*Today was foggy.*"), an event ("*Brent's puppy visited us today.*"), minor disasters ("*A pitcher of milk spilled at snack time.*"), or even food ("*We made gingerbread cookies this morning.*"). At the end of the month, read the calendar comments back to children, and discuss the past days and events.

September

SUNDAY	MONDAY	TUESDAY	WEDNESDAY	THURSDAY	FRIDAY	SATURDAY
1	2 Sunny Day	3 Hamster had babies	4 Sara's birthday	5 Rain	6 cookies for snack	7
8	9 Sang Old MacDonald	10 played baseball today	11 cloudy	12 Learned a new song	13 Visit from Firemen	14
15	16 made orange juice	17 Hana's birthday	18 Trip to police station	19 Had gym today	20 Saw a rainbow	21
22	23 puppet show	24 Sunny day	25 red day	26 windy day	27 baked a cake	28
29	30 apples for snack					

● Help children make clocks from paper plates. Help them print the hours around the plates' edges with a marker. Help them to make cardboard hands and to fasten the hands to the center of the plate with a fastener. Discuss with children the hours of the day and activities that happen at different times.

Language Development

● List as many favorite activities as your group can think of. Then take a pasteboard and divide it in half with a black marker. Title one half, "What Happens at Night," and illustrate it with a picture of the moon. Title the other half, "What Happens During the Day," and illustrate it with a picture of the sun. Ask children to help you divide the activities and list them under the proper heading. Ask children which activities can be listed under both headings.

● Talk about night noises with children. If possible, go on a moonlight hike with the children and their parents. Ask children about the sounds they hear. Have children create poems of silly words and noises they hear after dark. Hang the descriptions and poems on the wall on a "poem tree."

● Read *Go Away, Bad Dreams* by Susan Hill (Random House), and talk to children about dreams and nightmares. Make a "dream booklet." Let children illustrate the booklet with pictures of their favorite dreams.

Music

● Ask children to help you sing familiar lullabies, such as "Hush, Little Baby," "Lullaby and Goodnight," and "Rock-a-Bye Baby." Have children cradle one foot and call it their "foot baby." Have them pat it, sing to it, and hum it to sleep. Have them lay their "foot babies" down very carefully and then rock the other foot to sleep. Remind children to talk softly so that their "foot babies" will not awaken.

● Teach children this song:

> The Sun
> (tune: "I'm a Little Teapot")
> *When the sun comes up,*
> *We start our day.*
> *Dress and eat our breakfast,*
> *Go outside to play.*
> *When the day is over,*
> *Sun goes down.*
> *Moon and stars*
> *Light up the town.*

Field Trips

Take children on two walks, one in the morning and one at night, over the same route. Invite parent volunteers to help to supervise children. Discuss differences in what is seen, heard, smelled, and felt on each trip. Look for diurnal animals and events, such as rabbits and busy traffic, and nocturnal animals and events, such as owls and glowing streetlights. Talk about the colors of children's clothing and how they look in the dark.

Science

● Set up a "time center" by displaying on a table as many kinds of time pieces as you can find. Ask children and parents to bring in unusual timing devices. Include watches and clocks, sundials, candles with hours marked on them, small timers, stop watches, hour glasses, metronomes, and chronometers.

● Read *Bear Shadow* by Frank Asch (Prentice-Hall). Explain to children that a shadow is a dark area that is made on a lighted surface (such as a sidewalk during the daytime) when an object (such as your body) comes between the light (such as the sun) and the surface. To illustrate, shine a bright light on a wall in a darkened room and ask children to take turns standing in front of the light. Let children have fun with shadows by making shadow pictures and strange animal shapes on the wall.

● Find pictures of nocturnal animals in books. Read about and discuss with children their sleeping and eating habits. Also talk about diurnal animals and their activities during the daytime and the nighttime.

● Help children make a simple sundial by punching a hole in the center of a paper plate, sticking a pencil through the hole, setting the plate in the sun, and using the pencil point to pin the sundial to the ground. As the shadow of the pencil moves around the plate, mark where it falls at the beginning and end of the day, at lunchtime, and at nap or quiet time. Show children pictures of more elaborate sundials.

● Have children make "telescopes" out of toilet-paper tubes. Tape two tubes together, or use one tube (children can close one eye and look through the tube with the other). Let them decorate the tubes with paint and markers and go "star hunting" at night. The tubes help them focus on a few stars at a time, making these stars look clearer and brighter. Make sure they only look through the tubes while seated or standing still.

Read Aloud Books

🔖 *Anno's Sundial* by Mitsumasa Anno (Philomel Books)

🔖 *Arrow to the Sun* by Gerald McDermott (Viking)

🔖 *Bear Shadow* by Frank Asch (Prentice-Hall Books)

🔖 *Bedtime for Frances* by Russell Hoban (Harper & Row)

🔖 *A Child's Book of Everyday Things* by Thomas Matthiesen (Platt and Murk)

🔖 *Clyde Monster* by Robert L. Crowe (Dutton)

🔖 *The Day We Saw the Sun Come Up* by Alice Goudey (Scribner)

🔖 *Go Away, Bad Dreams!* by Susan Hill (Random House)

🔖 *Good Morning. Sun's Up.* by Stewart Beach (Scroll Press)

🔖 *In Shadowland* by Mitsumasa Anno (Orchard Books)

🔖 *Lily Takes a Walk* by Satoshi Kitamura (Dutton)

🔖 *The Midnight Farm* by Reeve Lindbergh (Dial)

🔖 *The Monster Under My Bed* by Suzanne Gruber (Troll Associates)

🔖 *The Moon Jumpers* by Janice May Udry (Harper & Row)

🔖 *The Napping House* by Audrey Wood (Harcourt Brace Jovanovich)

🔖 *Sleepy Book* by Charlotte Zolotow (Harper & Row)

🔖 *The Sun Is a Star* by Sune Engelbrektson (Holt, Rinehart and Winston)

🔖 *The Sun's Asleep Behind the Hill* by Mirra Ginsburg (Greenwillow Books)

🔖 *Sun's Up* by Teryl Euvremer. (Crown)

🔖 *Switch on the Night* by Ray Bradbury (Pantheon)

🔖 *There's Something in My Attic* by Mercer Mayer (Dial)

🔖 *What Makes Day and Night* by Franklyn Branley (Crowell)

🔖 *What Was That?* by Bradley Mathews (Golden Press)

🔖 *Winter Harvest* by Jane Aragon (Little, Brown)

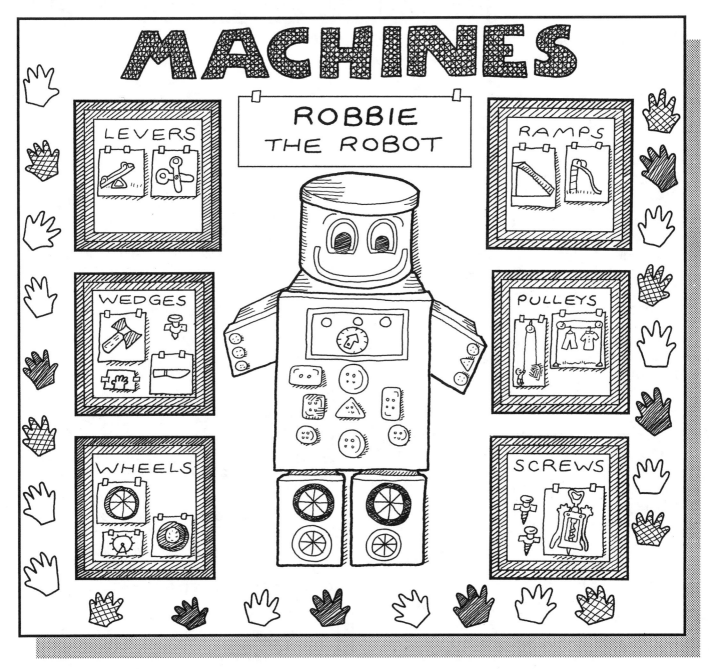

Machines serve many functions in our society. Children should be aware of the variety of machines we encounter in our everyday activities. This unit focuses on six simple machines and how they are integrated into more complex machines.

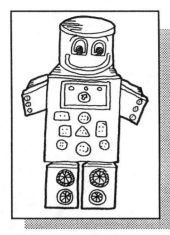

Background

One suggestion for the background is to cover the bulletin board with metallic paper, mylar, or foil. You can also use sheets of construction paper in bold, exciting colors. Or try alternating a combination of colors, such as red, yellow, black, and white. Another idea is to make different sections of the bulletin board different colors, or or to put colored rectangles of diminishing size inside one another.

Border

Since our hands are "human machines," the border can be made of children's handprints traced on colored paper and cut out with your help. On the top border put the title of the display, "Machines," in big letters contrasting with the background.

Bulletin Board

● Divide the bulletin board into seven main sections, one in the middle and six around the sides. Use the six side areas to display pictures and examples of each of the six basic machines presented in this unit: the lever, the wedge, the wheel, the ramp, the pulley, and the screw. Caption each section with the name of one machine category, using bold capital letters in colors that contrast with the background. When you introduce children to the six basic machines, tell them that machines are human-made devices that have moveable parts and do work for us. Some machines are run by motors, and others are driven with muscle power. All complicated machines are based on one or more of these six basic ones.

The **Lever** is a bar or a rod that lifts. It can be a beam, a stick, or a rod and something for it to pivot on. Examples are a crowbar, a seesaw, and even a broom. A scissors contains two levers.

The **Wedge** is an inclined plane that pushes things apart. Examples are a nail, a needle, an axe, a chisel, a razor blade, and a knife. Usually, a wedge is a thin piece of wood or metal with sloping sides.

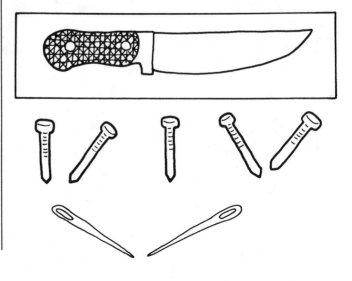

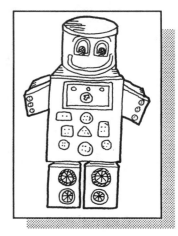

The **Wheel** is one of humanity's greatest inventions! All of our transportation depends on wheels. A wheel and an axle (which connects the wheel to whatever it is supposed to transport) make up a single unit. Examples of wheels are a tire, a train wheel, and a gear, which is a wheel with teeth.

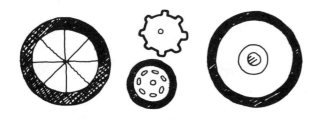

The **Ramp** is a flat surface with one end higher than the other, also called an inclined plane. A ramp makes moving a heavy object from one level to another easier. Examples are a slide, a garage ramp, and a staircase.

The **Pulley** is a weight-lifting machine. It is a wheel with a groove around the edge in which a rope or a chain is placed. Examples of pulleys include: an elevator, a hay-lift, and a block and tackle.

The **Screw** is a fastener with a spiral ridge around it and a sharp, nail-like point that is secured by turning it around and around, driving it deeper and deeper into the objects you want to fasten together.

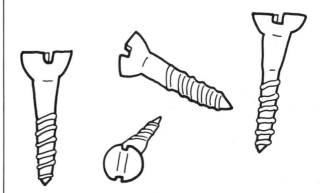

● Help children construct a large robot, captioned "Robbie the Robot," in the center section of the bulletin board. Use a large shirt box for the body, a hat box for the head, and four shoe boxes for the arms and legs. Take the lids off, and attach the boxes, open ends out, to the bulletin board in the shape of the robot using tacks, staples, or glue. Have children decorate the lids of the boxes with silver foil and macaroni, buttons, dried beans, etc. for knobs and switches. When the lids are finished, put them back on the boxes. As children learn more about the function of each of the six basic machines, they can add their drawings to the inside of each box. Or you can draw machine parts on paper and glue them inside the boxes.

Make the robot as simple or as complicated as children desire. The project should be exciting and stimulating but not frustrating.

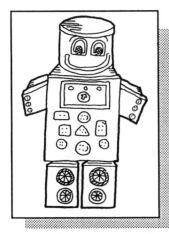

• Focus on one basic machine each day. Find as many examples of each as possible, and tape or glue them to the bulletin board.

• Have children make their own drawings of machines, real or imaginary. Encourage them to incorporate in their drawings one or more of the six basic machines. Frame the pictures with brightly colored construction paper, and put them up around the bulletin board.

• Help children decide how the basic machines can be incorporated in Robbie the Robot. Small round containers can be placed inside Robbie's "body" as wheels or cogs. Wrap cord around some of the containers to make pulleys, glue them to the board around the robot, and tie the cord to the "arm" and "leg" boxes. Pretend that these help raise and lower Robbie's arms and legs. Drive screws and wedges (nails) in Robbie's arms, legs, body, and head to look as if the fasteners hold the robot's parts together.

Inside Robbie the Robot

• Using the illustrations of the six basic machines mounted on the board, stage a scavenger hunt. In advance, put out objects with parts held together by screws or wedges (nails); toy cars with wheels; a stair or ramp (inclined plane); a pulley clothesline; etc. Divide children into six teams, giving each team the picture of one of the basic machines from the bulletin board. Set your timer, allowing them ten minutes to scan the classroom or the playground and come back with as many examples of that machine as they can find.

• Have children make up a story about Robbie during circletime, and let them draw pictures of some of the wonderful things the robot can do. Put the pictures around the bulletin board and connect them to Robbie with long pieces of "wire" (gray yarn).

• Have children sit in front of the bulletin board and review the tools and machines you have learned about. Tell them that there is one very important tool which we always carry around with us. Remind them that their hands are "human machines," and that is why the border of their "Machines" display is made of their handprints. Have children name some of the different things they can do with their hands, such as clap, wave to a friend, pinch a ball of clay, and pick things up. Then ask children, "*Which finger do you think is your most important finger?*" Hold up your thumb, and demonstrate its importance by encouraging children to try to pick up small objects without using their thumbs.

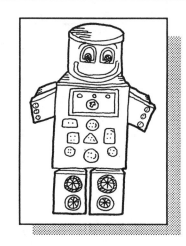

Art

• Help children make a "thing machine" from odds and ends of wooden scraps and other "junk" found on walks. Glue the scraps together at odd angles to make a huge machine, and let children decide what the machine's purpose is.

• Collect pictures of machines from magazines, and let children cut or tear them into parts. As a group, glue the parts onto a large pasteboard, making a montage of machine parts. Decide what the giant machine does, and give it a name.

• Help children make a robot from a cardboard shoe box. Tape the lid in place, cut a door in it, and fasten the innards of an old clock inside. Let children open the door to watch the gears work. Add a paper cup head to the robot and give it a happy smile! Let children invent imaginary tasks the robot can perform.

pieces of an old clock

• Have children make prints from machine parts. Show them how to use small wheels and cogs as stamps that they dip in thinned tempera paint and print on paper. They can also make prints with screws or nails (wrap the pointed ends in masking tape or clay), using the heads as stamps.

Cooking

• **Kitchen Tools** Take children on a tour of a kitchen, and list all of the kinds of machines and tools that are used in preparing meals.

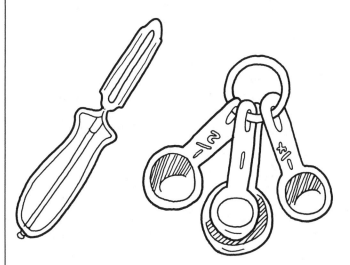

• **Magical Machine Cake** Prepare a package of yellow cake mix. Pour the batter into a well-greased square cake pan, a muffin tin, and several small aluminum loaf pans. Bake as directed. While the cake is cooling, make frosting and let children decide what color it should be. Use food coloring to color the frosting. Frost the square cake, and use it as the base of the machine. Frost and add the other shapes for wheels, levers, and gears. These can be cut into odd geometric shapes beforehand. Finish the machine with miniature marshmallows, raisins, candy sprinkles, and cereal as rivets, nails, dials, and starter buttons. Let children decide what the machine can do. Be sure to photograph the cake before children eat it, and put the photograph on the bulletin board.

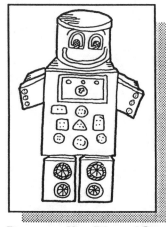

Dramatic Play/Creative Movement

● Have children pretend to be machines. Ask children, *"What would you like your machine to do? What parts of your machine move first? Does your machine make a sound?"* After each child describes her machine, have children all stand together, pretending to be a complex machine with many parts, each with its own motion. Ask each "machine part" to make a special noise. Choose a child to be a machine part that "breaks down." Have children demonstrate how one broken part affects the whole machine.

● Make a "circle machine." Have children stand in a circle. Start by making a movement and a sound. The child next to you should copy your movement and add another movement and sound. The next child should repeat your movement and sound and those of the child next to him, and then add his own. Go around the circle increasing the number of movements and sounds. If children find this too difficult, change the machine. Begin with a new movement and a new sound, repeat it, and have the child next to you add another movement and sound. You repeat the child's movement and sound, and then repeat your own. Go around the circle, asking each child for a new movement and sound, which you then repeat along with all of the previous ones.

● Have a child pantomime the act of using a tool, such as pushing down a stapler; typing a letter with a typewriter; drilling a rock with a jackhammer; cutting a log with a saw; playing a game with a computer; etc. Let others try to guess what the child is doing and what kind of tool is being used.

● Teach children this finger play, letting them make up actions for it:

Machines
I am a little machine,
And these are the sounds I make:
Putt, putt,
Plink, plank,
Round and round,
Crink, crank,
Ring-a-ling,
Slip, slap, slide
Junkety, jingly,
Rattle, rattle...
BOOM!

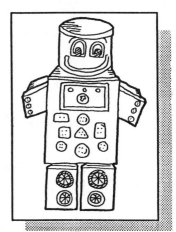

Language Development

● Show children pictures of airline pilots, bankers, fire fighters, teachers, computer programmers, etc. Ask them what special tools these people require in their jobs. Invite people with different occupations to visit the center and to show children the tools of their trades. Invite people who make or repair things, such as potters, tailors, artists, plumbers, carpenters, and mechanics.

● Make a "time machine" from a refrigerator box. Have children decorate the box inside and out, sit inside, and tell stories about the imaginary places to which they would travel. Be sure they describe sounds, temperatures, and smells as well as sights.

● Talk with children about how machines make our lives easier. Ask children, "*What machines in your home do you and your family use the most?*" After the discussion, invite some parents to come to the center for interviews. Make a list of their favorite or most frequently used machines, and include the results in a parent newsletter.

● Give children paper and markers, and have them draw magical machines that do anything they want them to do. The machines might clean dirty children without using water or follow children around cleaning up their messes. Help children give the machines names and make up stories about them.

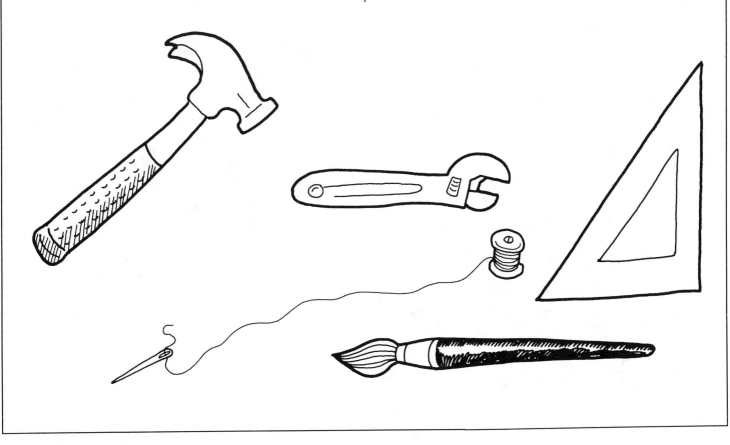

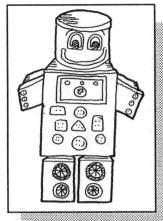

Math

● Look through magazines for colorful pictures of machines. Cut the pictures out, glue them to cardboard, and cut them into pieces. Let children use the cut-up pictures as puzzles, and try to put them together.

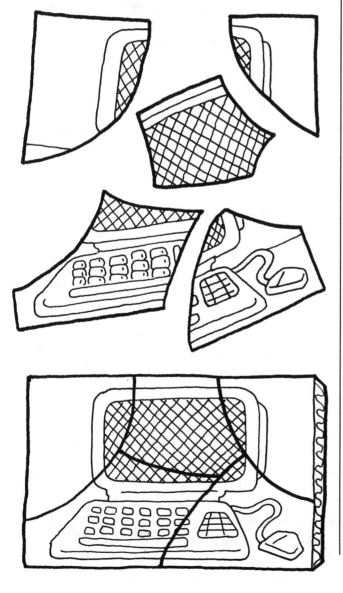

● Cut out triangles and rectangles from heavy paper. Say to children, "*Wheels are shaped like circles. What shapes can you see in other types of machines?*" Have them look at pictures of machines, and encourage them to find basic shapes in these pictures.

Music

● Organize a "machine band" to play and sing favorite songs. Give each child a simple tool or machine to make sounds—a washboard, an egg beater, a jar with a lid, etc. As children march around the room "playing" their machine instruments, have them pretend to be robots, moving mechanically.

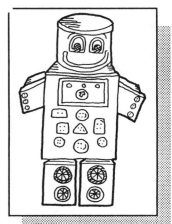

Science

• Take children on a discovery walk to find simple, everyday machines. Look at kitchen utensils and toys to find examples of each kind of machine—the fulcrum of the seesaw, the ramp of the playground slide, the wheels of a wagon, the pulley of a well, the gears of a clock, etc. Talk about the function of each machine.

• Have children build a "marble racetrack" by taping cardboard tubes together at odd angles. Add paper funnels to join some of the tubes, and fasten the maze to a board. Invent different games with the racetrack. For example, have children let a large marble and a small one go through the course at the same time, and see which one finishes first.

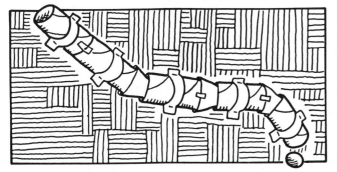

• Help children take apart an old telephone, clock or broken toy to see what makes it work. Have children identify machine parts, such as a cog, a lever, etc.

• Hunt for unusual tools at flea markets and display them on a table at school. Ask children to guess the function of each tool. Include a washboard, an apple corer, a tire jack, a bicycle pump, a potato peeler, a bottle opener, a spinning wheel, an air pump, etc.

• From a local body shop, borrow some hubcaps, wheels, a carburetor, a steering wheel, and other car parts that are safe for children to handle. Include wrenches and, if possible, a creeper (to slide under cars). Set up a body shop in class, letting children pretend to repair the undersides of tables, desks, tricycles, and wagons.

• Set up stations with different tools and machines at each one, and let children examine them. One station might have a hammer, nails and a crowbar. Others might have an old typewriter; a stapler with paper; a dust pan and broom; a ruler, a compass, and paper; an egg beater with a bowl full of water; or pencils, scissors, and paper. Be sure there is ample adult supervision at each station. Teachers or volunteer parents should oversee the activities to make sure there are no accidents. Change tools and machines often.

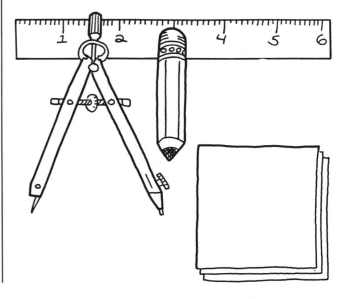

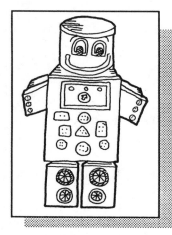

Field Trips

Take children to a factory, a hardware store, a farm implement store, a garage, or a body shop to observe the kinds of machines people use every day. Also take a trip to a science museum with children to learn about the history and development of machines.

Records

♫ *Moving* (Educational Activities)
♫ *We All Live Together*, Vol. 3 (Youngheart Records)

Read Aloud Books

🐀 *The Laziest Robot in Zone One* by Lillian and Phoebe Hoban (Harper & Row)
🐀 *Machines and How They Work* by Harvey Weiss (Thomas Y. Crowell)
🐀 *The Marvelous Mud Washing Machine* by Patty Wolcott (Scholastic, Inc.)
🐀 *Ready-Set-Robot* by Lillian and Phoebe Hoban (Harper & Row)
🐀 *Robot* by Jan Pienkowski (Delacorte Press)
🐀 *Simple Machines and How They Work* by Elizabeth Sharp (Random House)
🐀 *Wheels at Work* by Bernie Zubrowski (William Morrow)

DISCOVER THROUGH YOUR SENSES

In any unit on science, try to capitalize on children's awe for the wonder of the natural world. While exhibiting your "Discover Through the Senses" display, don't burden children with scientific explanations. They find magic in observing gravity, magnetism, reproduction, and growth. Children may not grasp the abstract principles behind their observations. Nevertheless, the experiments and activities in this unit will help children later when they study these abstract concepts.

Tell children that experiments have an element of chance in them. Like any amateur scientist, you will probably forget to account for certain variables in your experiments. Don't worry—successes sometimes happen in unexpected ways!

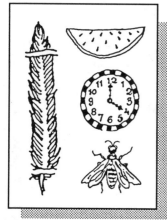

Background

Make the background flashy so children will know that this is an exciting unit! Bright red construction paper, slick paper, and glossy wrapping paper all make good backgrounds. You could also use shiny metallic wallpaper. If you are using very bright or neon colors, you will want to keep the design of the bulletin board simple. The slick, glossy, brightly colored background will provide enough excitement.

Border

The border for this vividly colored bulletin board should be eye-catching yet simple. Four-inch-wide strips of construction or wall paper in a contrasting color to your background would frame the display nicely. Make "miter joints" in the corners by beveling the edges of the strips to form ninety-degree corners when fit together. Add more mystery to the board by covering the border with question marks that children draw on squares of paper.

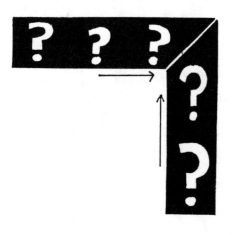

Bulletin Board

• Staple the title, "Discover Through the Senses," to the top of the board, using aluminum-foil letters.

• On one part of the bulletin board, mount an oversized picture—an art reproduction, a science poster, a plant or animal poster, or an enlarged photograph of a classroom event. Cover the picture with sheets of various colored construction paper. Cut doors in the sheets so children can open the flaps and see parts of the picture.

• Make a "Things I Like to Touch" collage by gluing or stapling swatches of soft fabrics, flower petals, velvet ribbons, acorns, buttons, elastics, etc. on pieces of oak tag and stapling the oak tag to the bulletin board. Put captions on the oak tag pieces labeling each thing in the collage.

• Mount pictures of things you can hear, things you can smell, and things you can taste on construction paper of contrasting colors, and put them on the board. Label each picture.

INTERACTIONS

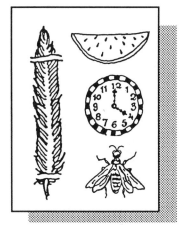

● Uncover one portion of the oversized picture each day by removing sheets of the colored construction paper. Then have children try to guess what the picture is before it is completely revealed. Change the over-sized pictures often.

● Bring in recordings of the sounds made by the animals and objects in the "Things You Can Hear" pictures on the bulletin board. Ask children to identify as many sounds as possible by pointing to the appropriate picture.

● Blindfold volunteers one at a time, and have them each touch one object in the "Things I Like to Touch" collage on the bulletin board. Let them try to identify the objects using only their sense of touch.

● Play smell-and-taste games to develop sensory perception. Fill small containers with cotton balls. Put different extracts, flavorings, or spices on the balls with which the "smell" pictures on the bulletin board correspond, such as onion, lemon, mint, etc. Help children to associate the different smells with the corresponding pictures on the bulletin board, and to identify the object associated with each scent.

Cut pieces of foods that correspond with the "taste" section of your board. Blindfold volunteers, ask them to hold their noses, and put the food samples on their tongues. Tell them to taste but not to chew. Ask children if they can identify what they are tasting without smelling it. Then have them taste the samples without holding their noses. Have them try to find the pictures on the bulletin board that show what they are tasting.

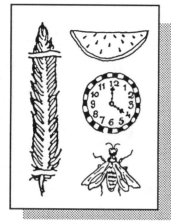

Art

• Make a three-dimensional display board from a large box. Use each side for a different scene. Help children cut out buildings, animals, people, or landscapes from old magazines. Group pictures of similar scenes together (a farm and a tractor, the ocean and fish), and glue them to the box. Discuss with children the ways in which all the pictures in a scene belong together.

• Create a "color explosion" with powdered milk, vegetable food coloring, and liquid detergent. First explain to children that powdered milk is made by evaporating (removing) water from regular milk. In a cake pan, add several drops of food coloring to powdered milk. Then add a few drops of liquid detergent to the mixture to make an explosion of colors which eventually results in a muddy-colored mixture. Discuss with children how mixing primary colors produces different colors. Ask them to recall what happened when you added the detergent.

Cooking

• **Magic Pudding** This recipe requires a group effort. Have everyone wash their hands and then stand around a table. Have one child open a box of instant pudding (I prefer the sugarless kind), another child empty it into a plastic bowl, a third child measure the milk, and a fourth child add it to the pudding mix. Cover the bowl and let each child shake the bowl. Shake a few more times for good measure, and open the lid. Children are amazed at how powder and milk become pudding. Spoon out portions for each child. Let them add their own toppings—granola, raisins, fruit slices, or sprinkles.

• **Fizzy Juice** Set out small pitchers of water, lemonade, apple juice, and orange juice. Ask children if they know why carbonated beverages fizz. Pour water into glasses, and ask a child to stir in 1/2 teaspoon of baking soda. What happens? Let children try the experiment with a small glass of lemonade. Explain to children that the baking soda has chemicals which produce gas in some liquids.

MAKING MORE CONNECTIONS

Language Development

● Glue a picture to a piece of construction paper, and then cover it with a second piece of construction paper. Staple together along one edge. Cut the top piece of construction paper into strips hanging from the stapled edge. Fold back one strip at a time, not necessarily in sequence, and let children describe what they see and try to identify the picture. Remind children that there are many parts of the world that remain mysterious until we take a closer look.

● Have the class "adopt" a nearby tree. Encourage children to record its changes each week with drawings and descriptions. Ask them to make up stories about the tree and the animals that live in it. Observe the tree throughout the year, and discuss with children the various changes it undergoes. Help children to understand that all living things—including children—change over time.

Dramatic Play/Creative Movement

● Let children pretend to jump in piles of dry leaves, in piles of prickly pine needles, and in rain puddles. Have them describe how it feels to jump in each.

● Ask children if they know what "gravity" is. Explain that objects fall because of gravity. Demonstrate by having children place blocks on imaginary tables, so that, when they let go of them, the blocks fall to the floor. Ask children, "*Have you ever seen anything fall up?*" Tell children that gravity is a force that cannot be seen, but that holds everything to the earth. Explain that balloons filled with helium float because they are lighter than air, but gravity keeps them from soaring into space. Have children pretend to lift objects of different weights, such as a bowling ball, a basket, and a feather. Have children get in a circle and pretend to pass around a heavy object.

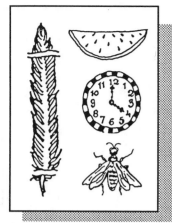

Science

• Cut branches from flowering forsythia and pussy willow bushes, and grow blossoms in your class. Fray the bottoms of the branches with a hammer, and then set the branches in warm water. If the blooming branches form roots, let children examine them, and then carefully plant the branches outside.

• Conduct a color experiment using a glass, a paper towel, watercolor markers, and paper clips. Tear the paper towel into three strips. Fasten a paper clip at one end of each strip. Using a bright watercolor marker, put a large dot just above each paper clip. Suspend the strips in a glass filled with 1/2 inch of water, allowing the paper clips to touch the water. The various primary colors in the magic marker dot will separate and run on the paper towel strip.

• Let children make a "mold garden" on a single piece of bread. Let the bread stand out in the air for an hour, put it on a saucer, sprinkle it with water, and cover with another saucer. Add a few drops of water each day to the bread. Tell children that the strange looking plants they see growing on the bread come from spores of mold in the air.

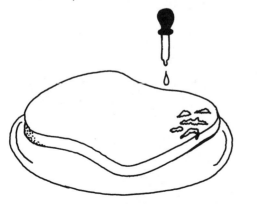

• Make a batch of "Silly Stuff." Combine 1/2 cup cornstarch and 1/4 cup water. Pour the mixture on the table, and let children slap it, pat it, and dribble it through their fingers. If the weather is warm, they can even walk through it. Ask children, *"What does this feel like? How is it different from play dough or salt clay?"*

• Make cabbage litmus paper. Boil red cabbage leaves. When the water turns dark purple, remove the cabbage leaves and pour the water over paper towels or coffee filters that have been cut into strips. Dry the strips. Explain to children that these litmus strips, when dipped into a substance, can turn either red (indicating an acid) or green (indicating a base). Let children dip the strips into all kinds of liquids—soapy water, lemon juice, milk, plain water, water with baking soda, and vinegar.

MAKING MORE CONNECTIONS

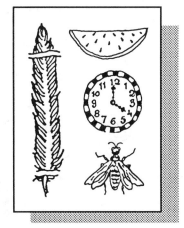

• Show children that green leaves have colors, in addition to green, which the green chlorophyll covers. Break green leaves into pieces and place them in a clear plastic container. Cover the leaves with fingernail polish remover (keep the remover out of the reach of children). Make a wick out of paper towel (about 1 1/2-2 inches wide), wrap one end of the wick around a stick, and lay the stick across the container top. After several hours, the wick will absorb the green color, and the leaves will show the colors the chlorophyll had hidden, the same colors that we see in the fall when the chlorophyll breaks down. (*Note*: this is a demonstration, NOT a hands-on experiment for children).

• Show children how to make a piece of thread dance. Unwind about eight inches of thread from a spool, and lay it on a table. Without letting children see you, rub a comb on your clothing. Wave the comb over the thread. When children ask how you made the thread dance, tell them that by rubbing the comb on your clothes, you excited certain particles in the air (created an electrical charge) that caused the thread to move. Let children take turns rubbing the comb and making the thread dance. Illustrate the same principal with balloons. Rub balloons on children's clothing and hair, and stick them to walls. These experiments work best in dry air.

• In the center of your science table, place a glass of water with a rubber band around the outside. Show children that the rubber band is at the level of the water. Have children observe the level of water in the glass a few days later. Ask them, "*What happened to the water; where did it go?*"

• Make a crystal garden. Arrange five or six pieces of charcoal in a disposable aluminum pan. Mix one half-cup each of laundry blueing (a rinsing agent used to counteract the yellowing of laundered fabrics), water, and salt with one cup of ammonia. Pour the mixture over the charcoal, soaking each briquette (keep mixture out of reach of children). Drip various food colorings on the briquettes. In two days, you will have a crystal garden to show children. Because the smell of ammonia is so powerful, combine the ingredients and pour the mixture over the charcoal after children have left the classroom for the day. They can observe the crystals two days later when the ammonia smell has dissipated.

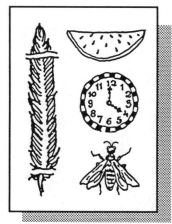

• Children can also observe crystals by making mixtures of sugar and water, salt and water, and powdered alum and water in disposable pie tins. Let children stir each solution until dissolved. Label each tin. Make two of each to allow one to be touched by children when the crystals are formed. With magnifying glasses, children can see the different-shaped crystals each mixture produces as the solutions evaporate. Let them compare these shapes with crystals in rocks you may have. Handle the containers gently—the crystals are fragile.

• Make a "magic wave machine." Remove the label from a one-liter plastic bottle. Pour in one cup of water and add blue food coloring. Fill the rest of the bottle with mineral oil. Remove as much air as possible by filling the bottle to within 1/2 inch of the top. Screw the top on tightly—you will have a mess if a child opens the bottle. Hold the bottle sideways and let children watch the waves. Explain to children that the fact that oil and water do not mix makes the "wave magic" possible. Make other "magic wave machines" in which you add glitter or crayon shavings.

• Help children make invisible ink. Combine four drops of lemon juice, four drops of onion juice (ask children if they know why onions make us cry), and seventeen grains of sugar in a saucer or paper cup. Stir with a cotton swab. Using the swab, write a special message on a piece of plain white paper. Iron the paper, or hold it over a lightbulb, and then show children what you have written. Pass out cotton swabs and paper, and let children write their own special messages to share with the class.

• Collect a number of magnets and let children discover which surfaces in the room attract the magnets. Categorize small metallic objects in the room as objects which can be held by the magnets, or as objects whose weight is too great to be held by the magnets.

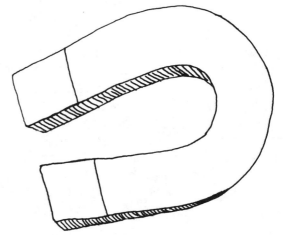

MAKING MORE CONNECTIONS

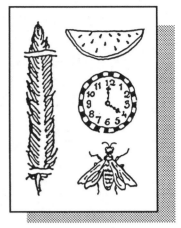

Math

● Help children make a balance scale from two aluminum pie plates, twine, and a hanger. Punch four evenly spaced holes along the edge of each tin. Help children hang a pie tin on each end of the hanger with twine. Hang the balance scale low enough so that children can reach it. Let children compare the weights of pennies, leaves, rocks, sand, etc. Let them balance the scales with pebbles on one side and blocks on the other side.

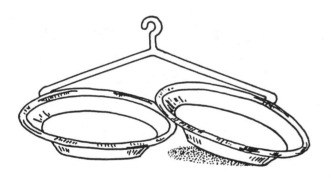

● Help children cut out pictures of buildings, animals, people, or landscapes from old magazines. Group pictures of similar scenes together (a farm and a tractor, the ocean and fish), and glue each group to the inside of a file folder. Discuss with children why certain pictures belong together.

Music

● Teach children this song about the wonders of our world:

Wonder at the World
(tune: "Twinkle, Twinkle, Little Star")
Wonder at the world we see,
DIscoveries for you and me—
Sun and moon and flowers that
  grow,
Mountains high and valleys low.
Wonder at the world we see,
Discoveries for you and me!

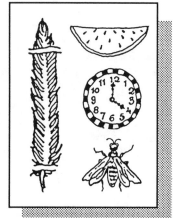

Field Trips

Take children on trips to museums, factories, or nature preserves to show them the wonders of the natural and human-made worlds. Children can also find examples of the scientific principles they have learned in the play yard or in the kitchen.

Read Aloud Books

🕮 *All Wet! All Wet!* by James Skofield (Harper & Row)

🕮 *Does Candy Grow on Trees?* by Karen Rice (Walker)

🕮 *Fascination Experiments in Physics* by Francois Cherrier (Sterling Publishing Co.)

🕮 *From Graphite to Pencil* by Ali Mitgutsch (Carolrhoda Books)

🕮 *Grandfather Twilight* by Barbara Berger (Philomel Books)

🕮 *The Great Science Magic Show* by Ned and Louis Arnold (Franklin Watts)

🕮 *Once There Was a Tree* by Natalia Romanova (Dial Books)

🕮 *Rainbows, Curveballs and Other Wonders of the Natural World* by Ira Flatow (William Morrow)

🕮 *The Seven Sleepers: The Story of Hibernation* by Phyllis Busch (Macmillan)

🕮 *Soap Bubble Magic* by Seymour Simon (Lothrop, Lee, and Shepard)

🕮 *Space and Time* by Jeanne Bendick (Franklin Watts)

🕮 *What the Moon Is Like* by Franklin Branley (Thomas Y. Crowell)

GROWING THINGS

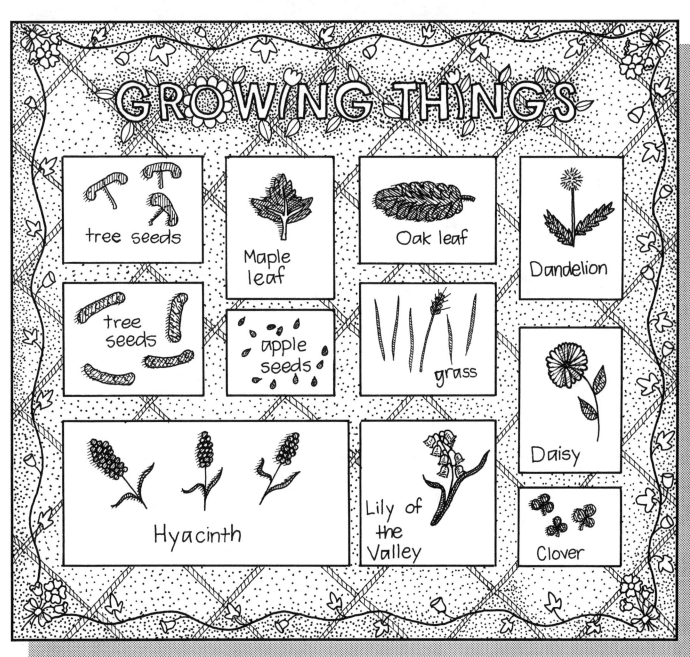

Children are fascinated by things that grow. Planting seeds and caring for the plants that sprout make children feel needed, capable, and important. This unit opens children's eyes to the wide variety of plants in the world, as well as to the beauty and usefulness of growing things.

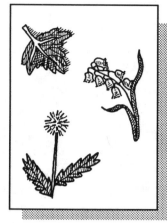

Background

You can make the background for the "Growing Things" bulletin board several ways. You can cover the board with a sheet tie-dyed in soft pastel colors, spatter-dyed white paper, or fabric sprayed with a food-coloring and water mixture. Whichever option you choose, help children do the spraying or spattering outside, clipping the paper or fabric to a fence. Have children line up with paint brushes or spray bottles and take turns decorating. The colors run and make the results even prettier.

Border

You can use paper leaves cut out by children from simple patterns (see **Interactions**). For a special touch, help children twist morning glory or wild grape vines around the board as a frame, and add a tiny nosegay with ribbon bows in each corner.

Bulletin Board

● To make the board appear more lively, evenly space tacks at the top and bottom of the board and crisscross white cord to make a trellis.
● Place a box or planter on the floor below the board for potted plants.
● Make a caption for the bulletin board of flower- and vine-decorated letters.

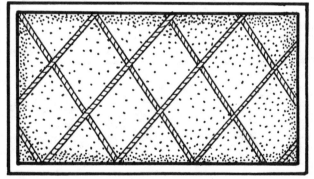

● If your bulletin board is in an area without much light, you can substitute artificial or dried flowers for real ones. These will last longer and make your board look fresh and alive every day.
● Another option is to use a window sill instead of a bulletin board for your "Growing Things" display, or use a combination of the two areas, putting live plants by the window and children's artwork on the bulletin board.

INTERACTIONS

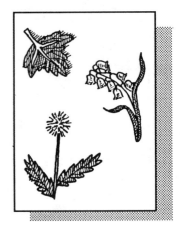

• Make simple patterns of different types of leaves, and help children trace them and cut out the tracings from orange, red, yellow, brown, and green construction paper. Let children make rubbings of distinctive leaves, transfer these to heavy paper, and cut them out to make the stencils.

• Have children draw pictures of the different plants and flowers in the "Growing Things" display. Have them use a combination of drawing and coloring materials—markers, water color paints, colored pencils, chalk, crayons—to reflect the variety of colors and textures found in the plant world. Hang these around the bulletin board display.

• Help children make a "touch it" nature collage on the bulletin board. Take them on a walk to gather leaves, pine cones, acorns, etc. Glue or staple these things to the bulletin board along with captions giving basic information about each object. Have children touch each object and describe the way it feels in relation to the other things in the collage.

• Help children plant herbs, small flowers, strawberries, or grass in unusual planters such as old sneakers, hats, and anything else you can think of. Line the planters with plastic and fill with soil. Plant the seeds and keep them in a sunny place, watering when the soil becomes dry. Display your unusual garden on a window sill or on a table near the bulletin board.

• Talk with children about the different things that help plants grow—sunlight, soil, water, fertilizer, etc. Have children draw pictures of these things helping plants grow, and hang the pictures around the bulletin board display.

• Using the bulletin board as a backdrop, help children create a garden in their classroom. Arrange benches, potted flowers, and a pretty pond (a small plastic wading pool filled with water, stones, and shells) in an area of the room. Add plastic or stuffed frogs, cats, rabbits, etc. to the garden. Play a recording of bird songs and other sounds of nature. Plan a picnic in the garden with children.

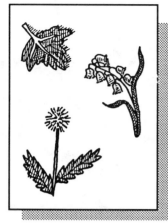

Art

• Have children make a flower mural. Spread a long sheet of paper on the floor and let children draw all different types of flowers and plants in crayon. When the mural is filled, cover the entire sheet of paper with a water color wash in any bright color you choose. Do several murals, covering each with a different rainbow color wash. Hang the murals on doors and walls, or on windows to let the light shine through them for a pretty effect.

• Help children trace around their hands on white paper and cut out the tracings. Show them how to make "Green Thumb Awards" by drawing happy faces on the thumbs of the hand cut-outs and each child's name on the palm of her hand shape with crayons, and then painting over the hand shapes with a green water color wash. Hang the awards around the classroom, or use them as place cards for a garden lunch party.

• Have children make "bean pictures." Give each child a piece of heavy paper and a small bowl full of dried lima or navy beans. Help children glue the beans to the paper in whatever designs they choose. Let children examine the beans under a magnifying glass. Then give them paints and paint brushes, and encourage them to create fantasy pictures around the beans.

• Have children take paper and crayons with them on walks and make nature rubbings of tree bark, stones, leaves, and other things they find. Take the rubbings back to the center and staple them together into a book-let. Add to the booklet after every "nature rubbing" walk.

• Help children trace around their feet on construction paper of different colors and cut out the tracings. Write each child's name on her foot cut-out in large letters. Tell children that these cut-out shapes are "foot petals." Help them make stalks of green construction paper and fasten the foot petals to the stalks to make "foot flowers." Hang the foot flowers on walls and doors.

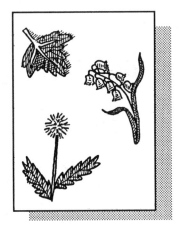

Cooking

• **Sprout Sandwiches** Put a few tablespoons of mung beans in a glass jar, fill with water, cover the top with a piece of cheesecloth, and secure with a rubber band. Let the jar stand for a few hours. Turn it upside down and drain. Rinse and drain the sprouts that appear twice a day and keep them in a dark place. Have children observe the growth that occurs each day. After five days, wash the sprouts and put them out with whole wheat bread, mayonnaise, cucumber slices, cheese, peanut butter, etc. Let children make their own sprout sandwiches.

• **Vegetable Soup** Bring in carrots, green onions, beans, peas, potatoes, tomatoes, and herbs. Tell children that these things all grow in the ground or on vines that have roots in the ground. Ask them to help make soup by scrubbing the vegetables. Chop three quarters of each type of vegetable into a large saucepan, and add chicken bullion and water. Cook over a stove until the soup is hot and the vegetables are tender. Serve for lunch with crackers or toast. Cut up the remaining one quarter of the vegetables and serve them raw. Have children compare the taste and texture of the cooked and raw vegetables.

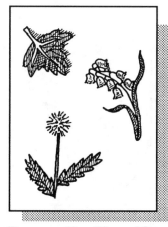

Dramatic Play/Creative Movement

• Have each child make a large construction-paper flower of either red, green, yellow, or blue. During circletime, have children hold up their flowers and assign one child to be the "leader." Let the leader call out instructions such as, "*Red flowers stand up. Blue flowers clap their hands.*" Let everyone have a turn at being the leader, and encourage leaders to come up with funny or imaginative things for the "flowers" to do.

• Help children make morning glory, daisy, or Queen Anne's lace wreaths. On a sunny day, take children with their wreaths outside to a lawn or field and stage a lawn dance. Bring a tape recorder and play some flute or violin music to set the mood.

• Have children pretend to be trees blowing in the wind. Tell them, "*At first you feel only a light breeze tickling your branches.*" Have them wiggle their fingers as if they were being tickled by the breeze. Then say, "*Now the breeze turns into a strong wind that makes your branches sway this way and that.*" Have children wave their arms as if they were swaying in the wind. Now tell them, "*All of a sudden, the wind turns into a howling gale that makes the trunks of the trees bend way over, almost as if they are going to break.*" Have them bend from the waist in all directions and try to maintain their balance. Finally, say, "*Now the wind dies down slowly, slowly, until it's just a breeze tickling your branches once again.*" Have children move their arms more and more slowly until just their fingers are wiggling in the breeze. You can also have children pretend to be a seed that grows into a tall sunflower.

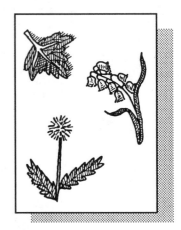

MAKING MORE CONNECTIONS

Language Development

• Make a list of as many occupations involving plants as you can—botanist, farmer, teacher, landscape architect, ecologist, etc. Share this list with children, providing an explanation of each job.

• Write the name of each plant in the classroom on a three-by-five card and attach the cards to the proper plant holders. Let children make up nicknames for the plants based on their real names, and write these on the cards underneath the plants' proper names.

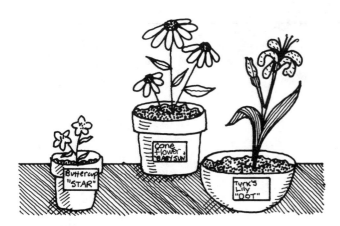

• Tell children that some people believe plants grow better when they are spoken to kindly. Choose two identical plants. Have children sing songs and tell stories every day to one of the plants while ignoring the other. Help them keep a chart to record whether or not the plant that has been spoken to every day grows faster than the one that has been given the silent treatment.

• During circletime, begin this story: "*Once there was a funny, red, fuzzy seed. Jennifer found it and planted it in the ground. Just as she finished patting down the soil and was turning to go, she heard a loud WHOOSH. When she turned around, she saw that something strange had sprouted. It was a...*" Go around the circle, letting children take turns finishing the story.

• Discuss with children the types of plants that might grow on other planets. Ask them to describe these plants using as many words as they can. Let them draw pictures of their alien plants, and help them write their descriptions underneath the pictures. Hang these up on a wall.

• Ask children, "*If you could turn into a vegetable, what vegetable would you be?*" Write down children's answers and put them together into a booklet. Let children illustrate the booklet with pictures of vegetable people.

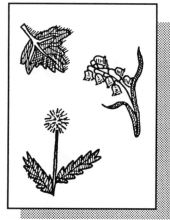

Science

• Have each child make his own garden by sprinkling grass seed on a sponge that has been soaked in water. Have them set their sponges on saucers and water their gardens each day. When their "lawns" have grown, children can "mow" them with scissors. Let them add small farm animal models and Lego houses to make farm scenes, or have them create their own scenes. Plant bird seed on other sponges and let children compare this crop to the grass.

• Take children on a walk and bring back some dirt from a field, an empty lot, or the woods. Put the soil into small pots and put the pots in a sunny corner of the classroom. Let children water them every day and watch what sprouts. Ask children where the sprouts might have come from.

• Use your herbs and flowers to make pot-pourri bath bags. Sew two squares of pretty fabric together on three sides. Make one bag for each child. Let children fill half of their bags with the herbs and flowers of their choice. Help them tie the openings shut with ribbon or a long drawstring tied in a loop at the top. Show children how to hang the bag from the bathtub faucet so that the warm running water flows through it and makes the bath smell sweet.

• Fill a pot with soil and plant a whole potato. Keep the potato in a sunny window and water it when the soil is dry. Watch children's reaction to the tiny potatoes clinging to its roots ten weeks later.

MAKING MORE CONNECTIONS

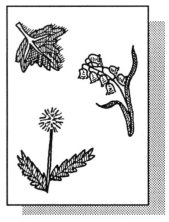

• Help children make a small vegetable garden in a bushel basket. Line the basket with a heavy duty plastic bag. Punch holes in the bottom of the bag for drainage. Staple the top of the bag to the basket so that it fits snugly. Fill the basket with soil, and let children choose what should be grown—leaf lettuce, radishes, green onions, etc. Keep the basket in a sunny window and have children water it when the surface of the soil becomes dry.

• Harvest some of the herbs and flowers you grow and help children make liquid soap. Mix a bottle of baby shampoo with one tablespoon of olive oil. Add a few teaspoons of herbs—lemon verbena or lemon mint, thyme, rosemary, geranium, and ginger are good choices. Have children smell each herb and flower separately, and then smell the mixture. Store the soap in a cool, dark place for about a week. Then pour it into small, interestingly shaped bottles. Tie a ribbon around each bottle and distribute to children as a gift. They can use it as a sweet-smelling hand soap or as a shampoo.

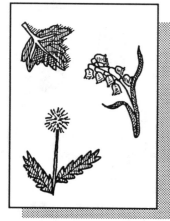

● Take a celery stalk with a good leafy top, cut off an inch from the bottom, and set the stalk in a glass with a mixture of water and red or blue food coloring. Put the glass in a sunny place and have children watch the colored water move up the stalk into the leaves—it won't take long. Point out to children the tubes that run up the stalk of celery carrying the colored water. Tell them that the plant uses these tubes to absorb the food and moisture it needs.

● Help children make a terrarium using an old fish tank, a glass jar, or even a bowl. Cover the terrarium with a piece of plastic or with plastic wrap. Put a layer of gravel and some charcoal on the bottom for drainage. Mix one part sand to four parts potting soil. Help children make little slopes and mounds in the soil. Let them poke their fingertips into the dirt and plant small ferns, ivy plants, or other plants that like heavy moisture in the holes. Add interesting small stones, lichen-covered twigs, and velvety green moss to cover the places where the soil is bare. Set the terrarium in a sunny place, but not in direct sunlight. Water the soil when it feels dry. Open the lid when there is too much moisture on the inside of the container. Every so often, clean out the inside of the glass with paper tissue or swabs. Pinch off plant shoots when they begin to crowd the terrarium.

Field Trips

● Take children to visit a greenhouse, a common garden, a fruit orchard, or a farm to see how different things grow.

● Go with children to a museum to see flowers and plants in paintings or other art media.

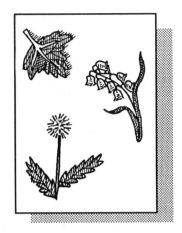

Math

• At snacktime, cut one apple into eight pieces, one into four pieces, one into two pieces, and leave one whole. Put two eighths together and compare to one quarter. Put two quarters together and compare to one half. Put four eighths together and compare to one half. Have children figure out combinations of eighths, quarters, and halves that will equal one whole apple in size.

• Bring in fruits that have many seeds inside them (apples and oranges) and fruits that have only one pit inside them (peaches and nectarines). Cut these open and have children count the number of seeds in each fruit.

• Draw a series of four pictures of a seed growing into a plant. Make the first picture a seed, the second of the seed being planted and watered, the third of the seed sprouting, and the fourth of the plant with its roots under the soil. Laminate these pictures and let children use them for a sequencing game.

Music

• Teach children this song about what makes a flower grow.

> FLOWERS
> (tune: "Are You Sleeping")
>
> I'm a flower, I'm a flower—
> See me grow, see me grow!
> Sun and rain together
> Make good growing weather;
> Don't you know
> How I grow?

• Teach this song about the growth cycle.

> THE FARMER PLANTS THE SEEDS
> (tune: "The Farmer in the Dell")
>
> The farmer plants the seeds,
> The farmer plants the seeds,
> Heigh-ho the derry-oh,
> The farmer plants the seeds.
> (Additional verses)
> The sun shines all day.
> The rain comes gently down.
> The plant pops through the soil.
> We weed and water and hoe.
> To harvesting we go.

• Have children sing this song about what worms do to help things grow.

> WIGGLE, LITTLE WORMS
> (tune: "The Farmer in the Dell")
>
> Oh wiggle, little worms
> And help our garden grow
> By mixing all the soil around
> While digging down the row!

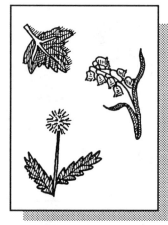

Read Aloud Books

- *Eric Plants a Garden* by Jean Hudlow (Albert Whitman)
- *From Appleseed to Applesauce* by Hannah Lyons Johnson (Lothrop, Lee and Shepard)
- *From Seed to Jack o Lantern* by Hannah Lyons Johnson (Lothrop, Lee, and Shepard)
- *The Giving Tree* by Shel Silverstein (Harper and Row)
- *Growing a Garden Indoors and Out* by Katherine Cutler (Lothrop, Lee and Shepard)
- *Herbs and Spices* by Julia F. Morton (Golden Press)
- *Outdoor Gardening* by Lydian Casey (Lerner)
- *Outdoor Gardens* ed. by Yerian, Cameron and Margaret (Children's Press)
- *Peter Rabbit's Gardening Book* by Sarah Garland (Frederick Warne)
- *Plant Sculptures* by Jack Kramer (William Morrow)
- *A Seed is a Promise* by Claire Merril (Scholastic)
- *The Vegetable Book* by Cynthia Overbeck (Lerner)
- *Vegetables from Stems and Leaves* by Millicent Selsam (William Morrow)
- *Vegetables in Patches and Pots* by Lorelie Miller Muntz (Farrar, Straus and Geroux)
- *Vegetables in a Pot* by D.J. Herda (Julian Messner)

LOOK UP IN THE SKY

Children are so close to the ground that nature's arched ceiling is a source of wonder and fascination to them. Encouraging a child's curiosity makes science and ecology natural sources of information about the world. Use the ever changing panorama of the sky to help children connect with nature. If possible, set up this bulletin board learning center close to a window, where children can observe and describe the how the sky actually looks. This unit is best done at a time of year when the weather is very changeable. The unit concentrates on sun, clouds, and rain, since these weather variables are experienced in all geographic areas.

Background

Help children create a soft blue sky background for the bulletin board by covering white paper with a thin blue water-color wash. The white streaks look like one kind of cloud. Tell children that these light, wispy, white clouds, high in the sky, are called cirrus clouds.

Border

Make the bottom border out of green paper fringed to look like grass. Border the other three sides with simple light blue or white paper to frame the sky on the bulletin board itself.

Bulletin Board

This bulletin board can be created over time as children observe the changing sky and weather patterns. Start with clouds and then add rain, snow, and rainbows as they occur or you discuss them in other contexts.

● Make a big, yellow sun to put in the "sunny" corner of the board. Paint a yellow or orange ball and add ribbons or yarn for rays.

● Help children make cumulus clouds. These are lower in the sky, and are the white, fluffy, rounded clouds that are so much fun to watch on summer days. Help children make these clouds from cotton balls. The cotton balls can be shaped like animals or objects—cloud creatures.

● Make one section of the board show an approaching rain shower. Help children create layered stratus clouds by rubbing the flat side of gray chalk on the sky. Position these clouds low in the sky. To show that these clouds are bringing rain, draw streaks with black chalk in the clouds, and let children smear it with their fingers.

● Paint rainbows that have soft edges by dampening paper with a sponge and then painting layers of water colors, wet on wet. Sprinkle the wet paint with salt to add even more softness.

● Help children make self portraits to cut out and place them in the "grass" on the bulletin board. Give them old magazines to cut out shapes of some animals playing in the sun and others with umbrellas walking in the rain. Add a few puddles for ducks and frogs to enjoy.

● Talk about the soft look of clouds, and ask children how they think it would feel to touch them. Set a small table in front of the bulletin board. Tape a sign to the front announcing: CLOUD TABLE. Furnish soft cloud play dough for children to manipulate and shape into soft forms. (To make Cloud Dough, mix 1 cup oil, 6 cups flour and pastel food coloring (optional) with a spoon. Knead, adding more flour if needed.) This dough is as soft as a cloud and very oily. Be sure to protect clothing and wash hands with soap and water after using. Keep the cloud dough in a covered container or plastic when not being used. Let children explore the qualities of this dough; poking, rolling, pinching, and pulling it.

● Provide old magazines with landscape photographs, such as *Arizona Highways*, *Ranger Rick*, or others. Collect photographs of clouds. Overlap, and glue them to a poster board as a montage. Try to find evening and night skies, stormy, dark cloud pictures, and summer sky pictures with soft, white clouds. Talk about the differences in clouds. What do the shapes and colors of clouds tell us about the weather? Post the montage next to your weather bulletin board. Have children try to match the photographs with the types of weather portrayed on the bulletin board display.

● Help children increase their vocabulary by becoming familiar with the names for clouds. Tell children that *cirrus* clouds are also called "horses' tails" and "white feather" clouds. They are the highest clouds, usually moe than three miles up the the sky. They are formed of ice crystals. They look like white streaks in the sky. The cauliflower-shaped clouds that are so much fun to watch and tell stories about are called *cumulus* clouds. They are puffy with flat bottoms and they change shapes. When they look ragged instead of puffy, they are changing into rain clouds. *Stratus* clouds are like wide gray blankets and are also called "sheet" clouds. They accompany drizzle or snow. *Nimbus* clouds are thunder clouds that are tall with flat tops. They lean in the direction of the storm. Make sure that all the many combinations of these basic clouds are represented on your bulletin board.

● Have a doll with an extensive wardrobe in a box near the bulletin board. As the weather changes, discuss with children how the doll should change clothes. This helps children become aware of why people dress the way they do.

● Read some weather forecasts from the newspaper (daily and long range) to children. Then create your own weather forecasting system. Observation is the most important ingredient for prediction. Explore *The Farmer's Almanac* for weather predictions and see how accurate they are. Here are a few farmers' indicators:

"The higher the clouds, the better the weather."

"When clouds look like rocks and towers, the earth will have many showers."

"When leaves show their backs, it will rain."

"When the forest whispers and the mountain roars, close the windows and shut the doors."

Art

● Talk about the fuzziness of fog, and tell children that fog is really a cloud that is hugging the ground. Paint fog pictures. Give children large sheets of paper and watercolors. Talk about the colors that can be seen in a fog. Are they bright or soft? Show children how to mute or gray bright colors by adding the complimentary color; a little red can be added to green, orange to blue, or purple to yellow to gray the colors. Experiment in making "foggy" pictures by drawing or painting landscapes in grayed tones, making soft edges on objects, and by brushing over the picture with a very thin wash of blue or white tempera mixed with water. Try also, painting "wet on wet," for soft blurred edges: dampen the drawing paper with a wet sponge, and plop on water colors with a brush. The colors will merge and blend with fuzzy edges.

● Help children make cloud monoprints by drawing designs in shaving cream on the table with their fingers. Demonstrate how to make the prints by gently covering the shaving cream designs with dark construction paper and patting gently.

shaving cream

● Give children pieces of sponge and a small tray or saucer of thinned white tempera paint. Show them how to make sponge clouds by pressing the sponge on blue paper. You could also provide other trays or saucers with tint; pale pinks, yellow, violet, and gray, and have children experiment with making clouds that reflect these colors.

● Take watercolor paints and white oak tag outside and try to mix the paints or match the sky you see that day. Children will be amazed at how many different "blues" can be found. You could also look at the cloud shapes and sky colors painted by famous artists, and wonder how they mixed their colors. Obtain a collection of paint swatches at a paint or hardware store, and bring them outside. Challenge children to match the colors of the sky with the paint samples.

MAKING MORE CONNECTIONS

• If rain clouds obscure the blue sky, you can still make exciting pictures. Rain drops can be artists. Help children drop small amounts of powdered tempera paint in several colors on heavy paper. (We like to use lavender, blue, and silver paints). Set the paper outside on the sidewalk for a minute or two, and let children watch through the window. When the colors begin to mix and run, bring the pictures in and let them dry. You could also let children paint thick bands of color on sturdy paper and set the pictures out for a minute or two. (Of course, heavy rain storms do not work well for this project. Drizzly days are perfect).

• Collect pictures of rainbows from magazines and mount them on a wall with pictures children have drawn. You may wish to draw pictures of rainbows and put them into a book with stories children have dictated.

• There are many types of rainbows. Moonbows are found close to coastlines that receive much rainfall. They are caused by the light of the full moon rather than the light of the sun. Tell children that moonbows are night bridges to the sky. Have children make pictures of moonbows on black or dark blue paper by folding the paper, unfolding it, and dropping thin white paint on one side in an arc pattern. Refold the paper and pat it. When unfolded, you should see a gauzy white moonbow. *Redbows* can be seen five to ten minutes before the sun sets. All of the colors fade except red. One doesn't get the opportunity to see them very often. Make pictures of redbows by sponge-painting rainbow shapes on paper in shades of red—from pink to crimson.

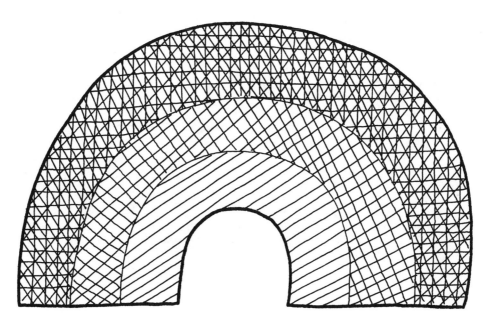

Cooking

- **Feast of Clouds** Give children time to think about and name foods that remind them of clouds. Make a list of the foods they can name. Ask children why those particular foods make them think of clouds (mashed potatoes, meringues, marshmallows, whipped cream, vanilla pudding, ice cream...). What words could be used to describe both the foods and the clouds? (*fluffy, soft, white, light, rounded, plump*...). Plan a smorgasboard and include as many of the foods mentioned as possible. Let children sample the foods. Vote on the food that tastes and looks the most like a cloud!

- **Cloud Meringues** Make these light and airy cookies by beating two egg whites, 1/8 teaspoon of salt, and 1/8 of cream of tartar together untill stiff. Add 3/4 cup of sugar gradually, beating all the time. Beat until the meringue dough makes stiff peaks. Let children drop the dough by teaspoonfuls on a cookie sheet covered with brown paper (or aluminum foil sprayed with vegetable shortening). Preheat the oven to 375 degrees. Turn off the oven, and put in the cookies. Leave in the oven until cool. (You can also bake the cookies in a 200 degree oven for 2 hours.) Do not double this recipe.

- **Rainbow Bread** Use a basic white bread recipe. Divide the recipe and let children choose several colors. Add food colorings to the liquid before mixing it with the dry ingredients. Have children pat the dough out one color on top of the other. Then roll up the sandwiched dough and bake it. Slice and serve the Rainbow Bread with pineapple juice garnished with ice cubes made of grape, orange, and cranberry juice.

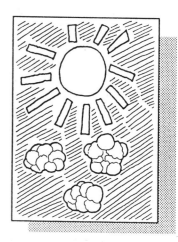

Dramatic Play/Creative Movement

● On a day when the noise and energy levels are high (perhaps, too high), choose a book or story about clouds or fog, and put children in a listening mood. Let them quietly tiptoe around the room, walking through fog or on a cloud. Ask them to sit back down, landing softly as a cloud might drop.

● Act out a rainy day with children. Use a small drum or pan and spoon to simulate the patter of the raindrops and the thunder. Let children pretend to be raindrops, thunder, and lightning.

● Begin a quiet time with visualization. Speaking slowly and softly, say, "*Think of something soft, something beautiful. Can you see something cool and blue? Close your eyes and pretend to be a cloud, or a balloon, or a single flower in a wide green lawn.*" Help children do some yoga breathing: breathing in slowly through the nose, holding the breath for a few seconds, and blowing the breath out through the mouth. Help children stretch and then relax all their muscles, one by one. Name each part of the body as you stretch and relax it, beginning with toes and fingers.

Math

● Keep a record of the weather conditions over a period of time and create a pictograph at the same time. Divide a large piece of oak tag into three horizontal sections. At the left, draw or paste a picture of a sun, clouds, and an umbrella in each of the three sections. Each day, decide on the predominant weather with children and add a copy of the symbol to that row. Each week, help children focus on the information on the pictograph with questions like: "Was it rainy or sunny more days this week?" "Cloudy or rainy?" Have children answer the questions first by just looking at the pictograph. Then have them count the symbols in each row to confirm their answers. You can do weekly charts and compare them or keep one chart over a number of weeks with a group who have worked on number skills.

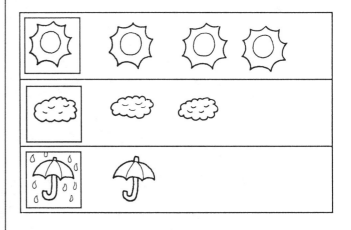

Language Development

● Read books about clouds like *The Cloud Book* by Tomie DePaola *(Holiday House)*, *Dreams* by Peter Spier (Doubleday), and *Sky Dragon* by Ron Wegen (Greenwillow), and then help children make their own booklets about the cloud shapes seen in the sky or in book illustrations. You could call the cloud creatures, "cloud walkers." Let children make up stories about the adventures of the creatures and illustrate them with cloud creatures of cotton batting and storm creatures of gray drier lint. Give children a variety of materials to use, and encourage them to be creative in their stories and illustrations. String a clothesline across one corner of the reading area, and hang the books on the line.

● Make it a point to check the sky color whenever you go outside with children, and talk about the differences in sky color and cloud shapes you see throughout the year. For language development, make a chart and help children supply adjectives to describe the color of the sky and the shape and color of the clouds each day. What differences do you see in winter and summer skies?

● Collect poems about the weather: clouds, sunshine, fog, rain, rainbows, and snow. Read them many times to children and then print them in a booklet for children to illustrate and take home to share with their families.

MAKING MORE CONNECTIONS

● Children love folk tales about clouds. I tell my children about people long ago in Europe who saw giants and castles in the clouds. In Labrador, it was sometimes believed that fog was a white bear that drank too much water and burst! Ancient Greeks thought that the moving clouds were caused by the wind stealing the sun's cattle (clouds). Native Americans often spoke of seeing thunderbirds in the clouds. We still see many shapes and forms and today we can also see modern clouds caused by jet planes! Tell some of these folktales at circletime and let children create and act out their own tales.

● Dewbows are special tiny rainbows that are easily missed if you are not an early bird. You can find dewbows on well-cut lawns early in the day. They are tiny horizontal rainbows formed on cobwebs of dew lit by sunbeams. Help children make up stories about dewbows and the tiny creatures that live in grassy homes.

● Many people have called the rainbow a bridge between heaven and earth. Tell children that long ago people were afraid of rainbows because they thought they were snalkes climbing the skies to drink water. Others called rainbows "the tongue of the sun." There are many folktales you can read to children about rainbows, the most fun of which are the Irish folktales that tell about leprechauns and finding gold at teh end of the rainbow. Let children make up their own tales about what might be found at the end of a rainbow.

Music

Music can change the mood of a room or a day. When children are jumpy or grumpy, sing about gentle rain or the stillmness of fog. Here are some easy songs about weather set to familiar tunes.

● This song is fun for children to move to. Ask several children to be clouds, and then appoint one sun, moon, and several stars.

Cloud
(tune: "There's a Little Green Frog, Sitting in the Water")
I'm a soft white cloud,
floating in the sky.
A soft white cloud,
drifting up so high.
The sun and the birds
are my friends each day,
The moon and the stars
sing the nights away.
I'm a soft white cloud
floating in the sky.
See you by and by.

● The Fog Is Creeping In
(tune: "Farmer in the Dell")
The fog is creeping in,
It slips beneath the gate,
Whisper, murmur, let me in
The morning cannot wait.

I'm walking on a cloud
It's soft around my toes;
The fog is all round my head,
I know not where it goes.

The fog has fingers soft,
They creep through morning trees.
The droplets on the leaves like jewels,
hang still without a breeze.
(Whisper) I walk with quiet feet.

● Rain
(tune: "Frere Jacques")
It is raining,
It is raining,
On my head,
On my head.
Pitter, patter, raindrops,
Pitter, patter raindrops.
I'm all wet.
I'm all wet.

Science

● Did you know that the sky as seen from Mars is pink, the moon's sky is black, and that Venue has a yellow sky? Astronauts tell us of the beauty of our earth as seen from outer space and have called earth, "Our Blue Planet." To give children an idea of why the sky appears blue to us, stir a few drops of milk into a glass of water. Darken the room, and shine the flashlight against the side of the glass. As you look through the glass, the liquid looks bluish, not white. The drops of milk have scattered the blue light rays. During discussion time, talk about how the drops of milk have scattered the light rays from the flashlight in the same way that water droplets and dust particles in the air scatter the rays of the sun. The sky looks blue because the blue rays scatter the most.

MAKING MORE CONNECTIONS

● Reflect the sky and see clouds twice! In warm weather, you can make a small reflection pool by setting a shallow pan or pool of water in an open space to reflect the beauty of the sky. You could also see the sky's reflection in a small mirror laid flat on the ground.

● Catch a pet raindrop and bring it inside to circletime. Give children a magnifying glass so that they can see their pet raindrop clearly. Notice its shape, not round so such as shaped like a hamburger bun.

● Tell children that rain comes from clouds made of water vapor. Droplets are so small that there might be a million droplets in only one raindrop or seven million in a tablespoon! Rain falls about six miles an hour when the air is still. Watch the drops splat on the sidewalk or catch them in a pan or can marked in inches for a rain gauge. Compare your rain measurement to the official ones in the area.

● You can even made some rain inside your center! Use a glass coffee pot half full of water and simmer it on the stove. Set a small plate on top of the pot and heap a few ice cubes on the plate. In a few minutes, you can check the bottom of the plate. You will find a collection of tiny droplets of water on the bottom of the plate; rain drops.

● Tell children that rainbows are caused by the reflection and refraction of the sun's rays in droplets of water. A small mirror standing at an angle in a glass of water in sunlight illustrates the way the sun's light can be separated into many colors. Rainbows are always located in front of a person who is standing with her back towards the sun. It fascinates children to realize that each of us sees a rainbow that is different from anyone else's rainbow because we are standing in different places and see different drops of water. Tell children that each of us has al rainbow.

● If you have a prism, you can create a rainbow on the floor or a wall on a sunny day.

● To make a rainbow outside, use the fine spray of the garden hose. Experiment with different locations, times of day, and water pressure. Talk about the conditions present when you see rainbows. We usually look for them when a thin misting rain does not completely hide the sun.

Read Aloud Books

🔖 *Air, the Invisible Ocean* by Sigmund Kalina (Lothrup, Lee, and Shephard)

🔖 *Bringing the Rain to Kaputi Plain* by Verna Aardema (Dial Press)

🔖 *The Cloud* by Deborah Kagan Ray (Harper and Row)

🔖 *The Cloud Book* by Tomie De Paola (Holiday House)

🔖 *Clouds, Rain, Clouds Again* by Lawrence Lowery (Holt, Rinehart, and Winston)

🔖 *Cloudy with Chance of Meatballs* by Judi Barrett (Aladdin)

🔖 *Exploring the Sky by Day* by Terence Dickenson (Camden House)

🔖 *Evening Gray, Morning Red* by Barbara Wolf (Macmillan)

🔖 *Flash, Crash, Tumble, and Roll* by Franklin Brandy (Crowell)

🔖 *How to Make a Cloud* by Jeanne Benedick (Parent's Magazine Press)

🔖 *Nimby* by Jasper Tompkins (Green Tiger Press)

🔖 *Rainbows, Mirages, and Sun Dogs* by Roy Gallant (Macmillan)

🔖 *Sunsets, Twilights, and Evening Skies* by Aden and Marjorie Meinel (Cambridge Press)

🔖 *Weather* by Julian May (Follett)

🔖 *Weather All Around* by Tillie S. Peine and Joseph Levine (McGraw Hill)

BULLETIN BOARD BRIEFS

If you've read this far, I'm sure you have ideas you can't wait to try—variations and adaptations of what you've read here as well as ideas of your own. The following section contains descriptions of other bulletin boards for you to create or to use for ideas and inspiration.

DINOSAURS

A study of dinosaurs is exciting and has dozens of applications in the classroom. It reinforces math, science, and language concepts. Although children cannot conceive of time and animals thousands of years ago, they can identify with dinosaurs because of their fossil remains. The mystery that surrounds dinosaur's size and extinction also makes them interesting to children.

DINOSAURS

Background

Cover the top half of the board in blue paper and the bottom half in green paper. Tell children that the landscape you are creating comes from the Mesozoic era—more than 150 million years ago.

Border

Make the top border an arch of giant, fern-shaped leaves, with branches hanging from the corners. Let children make the bottom border by stamping prints of dinosaur tracks (*how to make stamps?*) along the base of the bulletin board.

Bulletin Board

● As children learn more about the sizes of different dinosaurs and where they live, let them staple cut-outs of different creatures on the board. Help children cut simple dinosaur shapes from oaktag or cardboard. Cover them with a mixture of white glue and water. Sprinkle salt (colored with food coloring) on the cut-outs to create a shimmery, reptilian look. Let children paint some of the figures with water colors. Tell children that no one knows what color the dinosaurs were.

● Let children add volcanos with red cellophane fire, vegetation, swamp trees, and smaller, more timid dinosaurs peering from behind foliage.

Interactions

● Help children paint a large appliance box and place it next to the bulletin board. Label one side: REPTILES OF TODAY. Collect as many pictures of reptiles as you can find, and mount them on the box. Label the other side, REPTILES OF LONG AGO, and attach pictures of dinosaurs. Label a third side of the box: IMAGINARY DINOSAURS, and attach to it pictures children make of dinosaurs from their imagination. Name these creations: "Messyasaurus," "Happyosaurus," "Cookiosaurus," and so on. Label the fourth side of the box, DINOSAURS TODAY, and attach pictures of fossils and skeletons from museums along with drawings children have made of dinosaur skeletons. Include pictures of paleontologists and their tools.

DINOSAURS

Making Connections

● Use thumbprints and outlines of hands to make dinosaurs. The thumb of the hand outline forms the tail of a Stegosaurus (with the addition of four sharp spikes) and the little finger his small head. Add more plates and details with markers. (Art)

● Take a trip to a greenhouse or nursery and show children plants similar to those that grew during the age of dinosaurs. Discuss what the climate must have been like in the Mesozoic Era. When you return to the classroom, create a dinosaur terrarium in a glass bowl or old aquarium. Choose miniature plants that need lots of moisture, such as ferns. Add small plastic dinosaurs and swamps made from small containers filled with pond water. If you have room, add a volcano made from an inverted paper cup. (Field Trip, Science)

● Take children outside and measure out the length of a dinosaur, putting a flag at each end and a chalk line in between. Fossil evidence suggests that a male Brachiosaurus measured 98 feet from end to end. (Math)

● Ask children what they would miss the most if they lived in the age of the dinosaurs. Write down their answers and let them add illustrations. (Language, Art)

● Go outside with children and look at the clouds for dinosaur shapes. Help them make up a story about the shapes you see. Clouds shift quickly so be prepared to change the stories with the cloud changes. (Language)

Read Aloud Books

📖 *Digging Up Dinosaurs, Dinosaurs Are Different, My Visit With Dinosaurs* by Aliki (Crowell)

📖 *The Big Beast Book* by Jerry Booth (Little, Brown)

📖 *Making Soft Dinosaurs* by Linda Bourke (Harvey House)

📖 *The Foolish Dinosaur Fiasco* by Scott Corbett (Little, Brown)

📖 *Dinosaurs: A Drawing Book* by Michael Emberley (Little, Brown)

📖 *If I Had a Dinasaur* by Ralli (More Singable Songs)

ANIMALS IN WINTER

Explore with children the ways that animals prepare for the cold winter months in the north. Children can learn about hibernation, which animals hibernate and why. Migration is another winter preparation which children can enjoy discovering. This bulletin board can help children answer the question "Where do animals go in the winter?"

Background

Help children create an autumn background by covering white paper with water colors in fall colors. By using broad brush strokes of red and yellow, children will create orange. By adding some green, brown will be created.

Border

Have children make leaf rubbings in autumn colors and cut them out for the border. Intersperse these with snowflakes, made by children. Show children how to fold square pieces of white paper first in half then in thirds and finally in half again. Let children cut random shapes out of each side of the folded paper, and then open the paper—a snowflake will appear.

Bulletin Board

● Help children create a large tree in the center of the bulletin board. The trunk of the tree can be sponge-painted on with brown tempera paint. The leaves can be torn from brown paper grocery bags and pasted on the bulletin board.

Interactions

● Help children learn about and create animals around the tree preparing for winter:
❑ Squirrels gathering nuts
❑ Bears preparing for hibernation
❑ Migratory birds waving good-bye before flying south
❑ Snakes and insects huddling under rocks and logs and in the bark of the tree

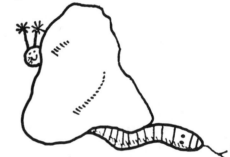

● Have children draw or cut out pictures of animals with white coats—rabbits, bears, owls, weasels— to add to the bulletin board. Talk about how the white coverings protect these animals in winter.

● Discuss with children the ways people prepare for winter, such as chopping fire wood, buying winter clothes, getting out sleds and skis, etc. Let children draw people preparing for winter and add these drawings to the bulletin board.

● When it snows, take children outside and see if you can find animal tracks in the snow. Can children identify the animals that made the tracks? Have children draw pictures of the tracks you find and compare them with pictures in books in order to identify them. Help them cut along the outlines of their drawings and add these to the bulletin board.

ANIMALS IN WINTER

Making Connections

● Point out to children how the tree and the area around it support many animals in the fall and winter. Make a list of the birds, mammals, and other creatures that stay in your area throughout the winter. (Science)

● Help children make a roly-poly bear from a brown yarn ball. Make the ball by winding yarn around your hand or a small book about 50 times. Slip off the yarn; tie a piece of yarn tightly around the middle; clip the loops with scissors; and fluff out the ball. Let children add features to the bear, making sure that its eyes are closed. Encourage them to find a cave for their bear to sleep in for the winter. It could be a coffee can painted in cave colors, laying on its side; or an upside down plastic jug with the mouth cut off and a cave opening cut in the side. (Art)

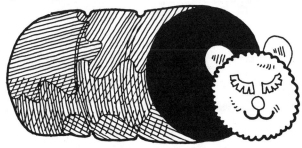

● Read *Birds in Wintertime* by Allen Eitzen (Holt, Rinehart and Winston), and take children on a bird-feeding walk. Give each child a small paper bag half-full of bird seed. Walk to a nearby park or playground, and show children how to scatter the bird seed on the ground. They will love watching the birds swoop down to join the feast. (Language, Field Trip)

Read Aloud Books

🐾 *Just the Right Place* by Jane Moncure (Childrens Press)

🐾 *The Seven Sleepers: The Story of Hibernation* by Phyllis Busch (Macmillan)

🐾 *Winter Sleepers* by Phyllis Sarasy (Prentice-Hall)

🐾 *Winter Sleeping Wildlife* by Will Barker (Harper)

🐾 *The Mitten* by Jan Brett (Putnam)

GEOLOGY

Rocks fascinate children and provide an infinite source of creative projects and learning activities. Children will discover the importance of this natural resource which can be found anywhere from a rock in the playground to the Grand Canyon.

GEOLOGY

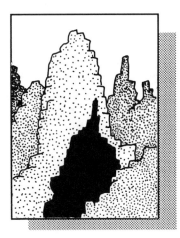

Background

Cover the back of the bulletin board with brown wrapping paper or have children paint a background in browns and grays.

Border

Help children create a border of rocks made of crumpled brown and gray paper glued or stapled around the edge of the bulletin board. Let children fill small brown paper bags with crumpled newspaper and tape shut to create boulders to attach to the border.

Bulletin Board

● Cut milk containers lengthwise in half and staple the halves like shelves on the bulletin board. Put one type of rock surrounded by moss and grass on each shelf.

● Put up photos from magazines or postcards or travel brochures of the Grand Canyon and other rock formations of the Southwest, sand dunes, deserts, and beaches.
● In one corner of the bulletin board, staple the shape of a giant magnifying glass made from paper or cardboard.

Interactions

● With the children, hard boil an egg. At circletime, slice it in half. Tell children that the earth is like a hard-boiled egg. The continents and ocean floor make up the outer shell (5-18 miles thick). The white is the rock layer going down almost 2000 miles. The inner burning hot layer is like the yolk, 800 miles across, and mostly made of the mineral iron. You can introduce some large vocabulary words that some children enjoy learning (*magma, core, volcano*, the names of some minerals) By cracking the shell of the egg, you can demonstrate how the large pieces of the earth's shell, called plates, were formed. They move slowly causing large land masses and ocean floors to drift. When there is a sudden movement, there usually is an earthquake.
● On a table next to the bulletin board display, set out large rock samples, a balancing scale, magnifying glasses, and sand. Let children examine the samples on the bulletin board and compare them to those on the table.
● Discuss with children how rocks are eroded (worn down) into sand by different forces in nature—rain, glaciers, ocean waves, etc.

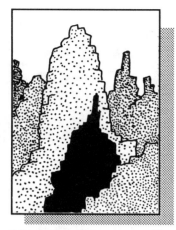

GEOLOGY

Making Connections

● Help children glue rocks together to make "Rock Animals" and "Pebble People." The smoother the rock, the easier it is to glue. A little cotton, placed between the rocks when gluing them, also helps to hold them together. Let children put features on the rock creatures with markers and scraps of fabric. (Art)

● Teach children this song about rocks: (tune: "Twinkle, Twinkle, Little Star")

Big rocks, small rocks, middle-size, too.
I'll go hunting rocks with you.
In the woods or on the hill,
We'll find lots of rocks, we will!
Rocks are magic, rocks are fun,
I'll find you a special one!

(Music)

Read Aloud Books

🖙 *From Swamp to Coal* by Ali Mitgitsch (Carolrhoda Books)

🖙 *If You Are a Hunter of Fossils* by Byrd Baylor (Scribner)

🖙 *Rock Collecting* by Roma Gans (Thomas Y. Crowell)

🖙 *Science Fun with Mud and Dirt* by Rose Wyler (Julien Messner)

🖙 *Sylvester and the Magic Pebble* by William Steig (Windmill Books)

🖙 *What Is A Volcano?* by Chris Arvetis (MacMillan)

🖙 *Volcanoes* by Franklyn Branley (Crowell)

WHAT'S OUT THERE?

Children love to talk and dream about outer space. Help them create an exciting "cosmic" bulletin board. Projects involving the sky and outer space can teach children about concepts of time, space, and distance while allowing their creativity and imagination to run wild.

Background

Make the background out of black paper. Let children flick white tempera paint on the black with a toothbrush to represent stars and galaxies. For an eye-popping background, carefully staple tiny, white holiday tree lights in arc patterns on the board before you cover it with black paper. When the board is covered, push the lights through the paper. When you have finished the bulletin board, darken the room and plug in the lights for a spectacular effect.

Border

Make the border a frame of aluminum foil or silver gift wrapping. The bulletin board should look like you are looking out the window of a spaceship.

Bulletin Board

- To make a moonscape, glue small items—macaroni, rice, bottlecaps—to the outside of a paper bowl or plate. Cover with heavy foil, then dab on black paint with a sponge or a rag.
- Let children create a giant sun for the bulletin board by dropping spoonfuls of thinned yellow and orange tempera paint on heavy white paper. Have children use straws to blow the paint into sunburst designs.

Interactions

- Show children photographs and realistic representations of the planets in our solar system. Help children make planets by painting circles with water colors and then sprinkling them with dry tempera powder to look like markings and craters. Make all the planets in proportion and encourage children to add details to each one that makes it unique (Jupiter's red spot, Saturn's rings).
- Help children construct futuristic rockets and space capsules out of odds and ends. First look at pictures of rockets. Then create cardboard-tube rockets out of tubes decorated in bright colors. Make the nose cones from circles of paper with a wedge cut out of each. Help children staple or glue the cut edges together. Finally, glue each cone to one end of a rocket tube. Glue or staple the finished products to the bulletin board.
- With children, sing "Twinkle, Twinkle, Little Star" as you work. Then teach children these new words to the song that reinforce the idea that the sun is a star.

Shine on, shine on,
Big round sun.
Children play and laugh and run.
When night time comes,
Your job is done.
Shine on, shine on,
Big round sun.

WHAT'S OUT THERE?

Making Connections

● Make a "star finder" out of a coffee can. Remove both ends of the can and paint the inside black. Cover one end of the can with cardboard. Poke holes in the cardboard, making a pattern resembling a constellation. Rub sandpaper over the holes to smooth them. Then cut a hole in the plastic lid large enough for the top of a flashlight to fit through. Put the plastic lid back on the can. Then put the flashlight top through the can lid and into the can, facing the cardboard cover. Turn out the lights in the room, turn on the flashlight, aim it at the ceiling, and watch children marvel at the constellation above them. (Science)

● Take children to a planetarium or to a space museum. (Field Trip)

● Help children take a Moon Jump. Measure out a six foot line on the floor with masking tape. This shows the length of a step an astronaut takes on the moon. Let children see how many giant steps they need to take there on Earth to equal one step on the moon. (Math)

● Try this action rhyme that gives children practice in counting backwards. To begin, have children sit with elbows close to the body, tips of fingers touching to form a rocket cone. Say:

Inside a rocket ship,
Just enough room.
Here comes the countdown:
10,9,8,7,6,5,4,3,2,1
And, ZOOM

When they say the last line, children jump raising arms as high as possible with fingers still held together. (Language, Creative Movement)

Read Aloud Books

🐚 *Arrow to the Sun* by by Gerald McDermott (Viking)

🐚 *Goodnight Moon* by M. W. Brown (Harper Collins)

🐚 *Home in the Sky* by J. Baker (Greenwillow Books)

🐚 *Let's Get to the Moon* by the National Geographic Society

🐚 *Moon Cloud* by F. Asch (Prentice-Hall)

🐚 *Nora's Stars* by Satomi Ichikawam (Philomel Books)

🐚 *A Sky Full of Dragons* by M. W. Wright (Steck-Vaughn)

🐚 *The Wind Blew* by Pat Hutchins (MacMillan)

🐚 *Regards to the Man in the Moon* by Ezra Jack Keats (Four Winds Press)

● There are two excellent kits you may wish to have, *Earth and Neighbors in Space* from Encyclopedia Brittanica and *Once Around the Sun* from United Learning. Both film strips and teaching materials.

SPIN, SPIDER, SPIN!

Encourage children's interest in spiders and webs with an arachnid bulletin board. Children can begin to learn that there are different varieties of spiders, only some of which are harmful. A bulletin board and activities about spiders can enrich children's interests in web weaving as well as storytelling.

SPIN, SPIDER, SPIN!

Background
Use light blue or black construction paper as your background.

Border
Have children cut or tear tree branches from brown construction paper or grocery bags. Glue the branches to the edges of the bulletin board extending inwards.

Bulletin Board
● Starting at the middle of the bulletin board, paint five concentric circles taking up about half of the board.
● Thumbtack pieces of black yarn from the branches in the border to the center of the board.
● Make a "friendly" spider with a happy face to put in the center of the bulletin board. Use two egg carton sections for the body and attach eight pipe cleaner legs, some of which should be waving to children.

Interactions
● Tell children that arachnids, unlike insects, have two body segments, eight eyes, and eight legs. Explain that a spider has very special openings in its body called spinnerets. The silk thread it uses to spin a web comes out of its spinnerets looking like milk, then dries to a very fine but very strong thread. Have children draw and cut out their own spiders from construction paper. Put these on the bulletin board web.

● Tack one long length of string for each child to the bottom of the board, and let children weave their strings around the room in a giant web, winding them around tables, cabinet doors, each other's strings, etc. Tie all the loose ends together. Have children crawl under and through their web maze.

SPIN, SPIDER, SPIN!

Making Connections

• Teach children the fingerplay "The Eensy Weensy Spider." (Music, Creative Movement)

• Tell children that different spiders make different kinds of webs. For example, the purse web spider makes a tunnel-like web on the side of a rock, digs a hole under the tunnel, and waits for insects to fall through the web into the hole. Help children make a tunnel web by dipping string into glue or liquid starch and winding it around a long, skinny balloon. When the string dries, pop the balloon, and prop the tunnel web against a rock. (Science, Art)

• Use the bulletin board to create "word webs" with children. Choose words from stories you read to children or words children bring from home and write them on large circles of paper. Attach the words to the ends of the large spider web. Try to use the words frequently for a few days with children until their meanings are understood. These words often become "buzz" words that children will use in every possible situation. (Language)

Read Aloud Books

🕷 *Anansi the Spider* by Gerald McDermott (Holt, Rinehart and Winston)

🕷 *The Very Busy Spider* by Eric Carle (Philomel Books)

🕷 *The Web in the Grass* by Berniece Freschet (Holiday House)

🕷 *Spider's Silk* by Augusta Golden (Crowell)

🕷 *Spiders Are Spinners* by Ellsworth Rosen (Houghton Mifflin)

🕷 *The Spider's Dance* by Joanne Ryder (Harper & Row)

🕷 *Charlotte's Web* by E. B. White (Harper)

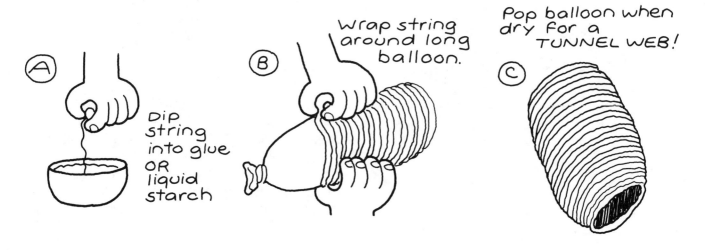

Ⓐ Dip string into glue OR liquid starch

Wrap string around long balloon. Ⓑ

Pop balloon when dry for a TUNNEL WEB! Ⓒ

WHAT'S GOING TO HAPPEN?

This bulletin board helps to make children aware of the sequence of events and that certain events "cause" other events to happen—cause and effect. The sprouting of a seed, the building and melting of a snow person, the baking of bread, all of these are examples of things that happen in sequence.

WHAT'S GOING TO HAPPEN?

Background

Cover the entire bulletin board with felt or flannel to create a giant flannelboard.

Border

Create a border with the theme of time. Have children cut out pictures of clocks and watches from old magazines or draw pictures of timepieces and cut them out. Glue the cutouts around the edge of the bulletin board.

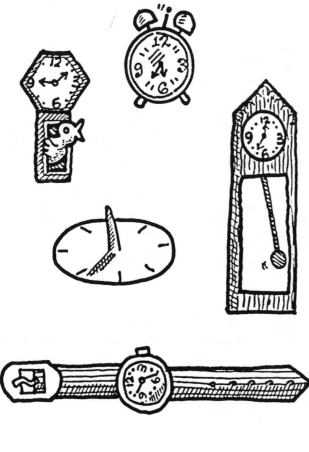

Bulletin Board

Create or cut out pictures which show a sequence of events and back each picture with felt or flannel pieces so that they will adhere to the bulletin board.

Interactions

● Ask children to help make pictures illustrating the step-by-step process of some activity they are familiar with, such as an easy recipe or an art project or a classroom routine. Glue the drawings to flannel pieces, then attach them to the board in sequence. Have children explain what happens by describing the pictures. Then change the order of the pictures; is the end result the same? Help children realize that the sequence of the events is often as important as the events themselves in order to realize the end result.

● Illustrate the plot of a story such as "The Three Bears" or *A Dark, Dark Tale* by Ruth Brown (Dial), and put the illustrations on the board. Ask children, "*What happens if the cards are switched, so that the events in the story are in a different order?*" "*Is it the same story?*"

WHAT'S GOING TO HAPPEN?

Making Connections

● Perform cause-and-effect experiments with children. For example, drop a ball, and have children watch as it falls to the ground and bounces up again. Discuss with children how different ways of dropping the ball to the ground produce certain effects. (Science)

● Introduce children to timelines. Draw pictures of a vegetable seed growing and changing over time, as it matures into a plant. Bring a camera to class. Give children a project, such as building a skyscraper out of blocks. Take pictures of each stage of the project. Let children arrange the pictures in the proper order. (Math)

Read Aloud Books

● *I Know an Old Lady Who Swallowed a Fly* by Nadine Bernard Wescott (Atlantic-Little, Brown)
● *The Milk Makers* by Gail Gibbons (Macmillan)
● *Peter Spier's Rain* by Peter Spier (Doubleday)
● *Rosie's Walk* by Pat Hutchins (Macmillan)